THE
BLUEPRINT
OF LIFE

BUILDING YOUR FUTURE
ON GOD'S MASTER PLAN

PAUL GRAHAM

DESTINY IMAGE™ EUROPE srl
Via Maiella, 1
66020 San Giovanni Teatino (Ch) – Italy

"Changing the world, one book at a time."

This book and all other Destiny Image™ Europe books are available at Christian book-stores and distributors worldwide.

To order products, or for any other correspondence:

DESTINY IMAGE™ EUROPE srl
Via Acquacorrente, 6
65123 - Pescara - Italy
Tel. +39 085 4716623 - Fax: +39 085 9431270
E-mail: info@eurodestinyimage.com
Or reach us on the Internet: **www.eurodestinyimage.com**

ISBN: 978-88-96727-04-1
For Worldwide Distribution, Printed in the U.S.A.
1 2 3 4 5 6 / 13 12 11 10

ACKNOWLEDGMENTS

A huge thank you to Anne Latz, my personal assistant, who has been an invaluable help while working on this book. Also, thank you to Teri Rowe for her assistance. Anne and Teri, without your help, the completion of this book would have taken much longer. Thank you both very much.

ENDORSEMENTS

Once again Paul has conveyed a cutting edge message from the heart of God. The journey of life contains opportunities for discovery of God's destiny for each believer. Paul reveals those opportunities as he unfolds his revelation of the apostolic ministry. He identifies with clarity and accuracy the spirit of the apostolic and not just the function. I would encourage everyone to embrace this core message and help redefine the Church and re-present the Kingdom of God to this present culture.

Pastor Louis F. Kayatin
Church on the North Coast
Lorain, Ohio, USA

Apostles who have a vision to build God's house and extend God's Kingdom are sorely needed today in God's world. Paul gets to the heart of the matter here. In contrast to those self-appointed apostles of some churches, Paul highlights that there is a process of growth and development of genuine apostolic ministries and apostolic people, and genuine character and heart qualifications. How does he know? This is something he has lived and walks in. This is not idle theory, but the fruit of his own life. I highly commend this book: in its pages we find God's heart for growing His own Kingdom people into their destiny.

Steve Thomas, Apostolic Overseer
Salt & Light Stream of Churches
United Kingdom, Canada, and Europe

It is clear that we are at a time of a new apostolic reformation. With the wisdom of many years of experience in the apostolic ministry, Paul shares many insights that will be helpful to this new generation. With his wisdom, it might be possible to avoid some of the mistakes of history and to see the church develop more and more along the pattern set out by God—reaching a new level of maturity that can bring greater hope to the age in which we are living.

Derek Brown
Apostolic Overseer KC21

The Blueprint of Life engages the heart of Christianity, and our Father's purpose for us individually and corporately. These are challenging, fast changing times in which the Church must embrace God's ways and means of harvesting those for whom Jesus died. The Body of Christ has for too long engaged itself with methods, rather than relationships. Paul masterfully brings us past titles and formulas, and reminds us of the relational qualities through which God worked so powerfully in the beginning of the New Testament Church. Religion did not understand; however, God used ordinary people and changed the world. Well done, Paul!

LeRoy Ede, Apostolic Overseer
Kingdom Dynamics International, Canada

CONTENTS

PREFACE

Recently I was asked, "If you had one opportunity in your life to print and publish something that you believed to be of vital importance, what would that book be?"

The answer: "This book that is in your hands."

It has been my privilege to write a number of books, but of all of them, this one, *The Blueprint of Life,* is the most important.

It is my belief that when Jesus calls us to Himself, not only does He have a wonderful future and destiny for us that will be a great adventure, but He also has a defined process and way of bringing us into the fullness of His life. This book outlines some of that exciting journey.

Oftentimes after we have come to know Him and begin our walk with Him, we get easily side-tracked. That's because He enlightens our spiritual eyes and we begin to see that there truly is a great purpose to our lives. At this point in our excitement to be "doing" the things He has set before us, we tend to forget that through all our doing He wants us to become more like Him, that our character, our heart, our inner being as well as our mind are transformed and conformed into His image.

This book deals with some of the journey into His blueprint for our lives, truly experiencing something of the fullness of who He is. Everyone whom He has called and all those who have come to know Him have set out on this life journey—His goal, though, is for us to experience fullness of that life.

JESUS — THE MASTER CRAFTSMAN

Jesus is the Master Craftsman. There is a way to build and reconstruct the person that you are into the person you were *created to be*. Of course you are incredibly precious—in fact, more precious than all other creation in the universe. Jesus doesn't play games with your life. He loves you and wants to build you; He has a future for you and a destiny that is beyond your wildest dreams. To become all that you can become, and for the Church corporately to become all that she must become, there is a process that He must take us through and there is a choice that we must continually make.

However far we have come, there is so much more that He has for us. He desires to build us in such a way that we can continually develop, grow, increase, and bear forth more fruit. The more we become like Him, the bigger we get! Not in our own strength, but through and in His love, life, and power.

As well as looking at the personal blueprint of life that Jesus has for us, we look at how our lives are intertwined and interdependent. This blueprint is for the whole Church as well.

PAUL — THE GREAT APOSTLE

In the New Testament there is a man named Paul who is now known as one of the greatest apostles. He talks about how he submitted to the call of Christ upon His life, and he too, like His Master and Savior Christ, was to become a great master craftsman. In fact, he modeled his life according to the pattern that Christ gave. This model and pattern (blueprint) became what he desired to pass down and model to others who followed him in the way of Christ.

> *According to the grace of God which was given to me, as a wise master builder I have laid the foundation, and another builds on it. But let each one take heed how he builds on it. For no other foundation can anyone lay than that which is laid, which is Jesus Christ* (1 Corinthians 3:10-11).

So, *an apostle is defined as a wise master builder or master craftsman*; he lays foundations upon which the Kingdom of God is established. Jesus set the example by laying down His own life to establish life for us in

His Kingdom, both here and in Heaven. Like Him, Paul became a master craftsman as he lived, taught, and preached about Christ and His life. As a result of this process, not only was Paul's own life built solidly upon the revelation of Christ, but he also built the lives of those around him upon this same unshakeable foundation. *Paul, the greatest of all the apostles, was a wise master craftsman.*

This book deals with the heart, characteristics, and life of a master craftsman and those "crafted" in His image. My hope is that it simply explains the apostolic lifestyle in such a way as to minister to leaders and followers alike. Since I am a simple man myself, I desire that both the well-educated and those less educated can find meaning and significance for their lives in Christ in these pages. It's only in Him that our lives make sense.

I will be using the words *master craftsman and apostle* interchangeably because in the sense of building, they mean much the same thing; thus *when I talk about an apostolic church or an apostolic people; I am referring to those set apart by selfless lives*—people who are giving themselves in love for God and others. Also, please note too that the term *craftsman* includes women as well.

> *The apostolic church or apostolic people are set apart by selfless lives*—people who give themselves in love for God and others.

When a person, church, stream of churches, or a ministry has an apostle serving and ministering into them, it's not so they can say that they are accountable to or associated with an apostle. Neither is it to give them credibility. Rather, it is simply that, according to the New Testament pattern, this the only way to bring the order and establishment of God's Kingdom into the earth's sphere in its fullness.

If the man or woman serving them in this capacity is truly apostolic, they will raise up a people who are also apostolic. They will mark themselves out as people who give themselves for one another; their lives will clearly be lived for another, namely Jesus, and then for His people.

As a result, they will begin to carry the signs of apostolic life. These signs include:

- ❖ Selflessness, or the giving of oneself to another in love.

- ❖ Meekness, the basis of all true apostolic authority.

- ❖ Wisdom, the foundation for building.

- ❖ Grace, for a sacrificial life of giving.

Furthermore, discipleship built on relationship leads believers through a progression from servanthood to sonship, eventually developing fathers—those who are truly mature. Although there are many other important traits of apostolic ministry, I have focused upon these particular aspects because I believe that they are not often spoken about and need to be brought to our attention once again.

Of course, when these traits are developed, then signs and wonders will also be part of normal everyday life. And beyond that there will be raised up new generations who, in themselves, are signs and wonders, doing wondrous things.

> **Apostolic Christianity is centralized and focused in the work of Jesus. Its central theme is the cross and resurrection of Jesus.**

Every teaching, every message given in the midst of the Church, should find itself in Him. There are many inspirational and dynamic messages being preached around the world. There are sound principles and formulas being taught; much of this is helpful to us becoming a better, more able people, more successful and prosperous, and all of this can be very beneficial, providing it finds itself in Him. If it is outside of Him and His finished work, in the end it leads to an enlarged ego, strutting of self, and pride in life, which makes *us* more, but does not make *Him more* in us and through us. Nor in the end will it bring glory to Him.

Apostolic Christianity makes us His sons, princes of the Kingdom, and ambassadors of His love and righteousness. It enables us to become those who have learned how to overcome the challenges of life. It does also make us successful and prosperous, but in terms of the Kingdom kind of success. It equips us to live in the world, overcoming difficulties, trials, and challenges, and at the same time prepares our minds to see in another realm. It helps us to communicate in ways that touch the hearts of others—being normal—and yet at the same time otherworldly, without being overly spiritual and religious. It puts to death old ways of thinking and behaving, and will have nothing to do with the "sinner mentality" and "miserable me" behavior. It's not part of an Old Testament covenant, although it has been learned and continues to learn from the Old Testament, neither does it allow us to live in the nebulous, in-between place of old versus new. No, apostolic Christianity learns and gleans from the old, as it sees it in the light of the new, looking forward to all that has been accomplished in Christ, all that He has made us to be, and all that we will yet become.

As well as looking at all these things, I will examine the concept of women in apostolic ministry. I realize that for many, these words may be enough for you to put the book down. If that is your response, I would encourage you not to be too hasty. I believe that there were women raised up as apostles in the New Testament, and that throughout history God has called, appointed, and anointed such women. I know that many are concerned with the issues of submission and authority. I also deal with these subjects in the chapter concerning this topic.

In the end, there is a great need not only to proclaim the truth, but also to see a life-altering release and impartation of grace, mercy, and love. We have often been good at dispensing the truth—but so were the scribes and Pharisees! But we have not as often been good at supplying grace, mercy, and love along with that truth. It is that same grace and mercy that will enable the people of God to begin walking in a new way, for a new day.

Walking in the world and living a Kingdom life is not always easy. There will always be challenges. Sometimes we will have to walk through painful and grievous experiences, we might even feel that things are falling apart on us; at other times, we may feel the intensity of a demonic battle raging—despite the fact we've already won it!

At those times, we need to know that the Master Craftsman has not given up on us. It is often in and through those times when we are being made more like Jesus. It is also very wonderful that we have those around us who have this same heart and mindset, because those who build from the foundations and see with those kind of eyes can bring great help, strength, and grace when we most need it.

In the Old Testament, the first chapter of the Book of Zechariah tells that Israel and other regions are under intense pressure with four kings coming against them and declaring war. When the prophet of God asks about this situation, the Lord answers by showing him *four craftsmen* who would terrify, cast out, and dispatch the armies of the enemy!

Perhaps we would have thought to send in greater and bigger armies, more tanks, and more war ships? But the Lord, He sent in craftsmen! (See Zechariah 1:18-21.)

God does not do things in the way that we think He should do them—but if we, His children, will give ourselves to the blueprint of life that He has for us, if we allow Him to take us through His transforming process, then we will understand and see the ways of the Lord in much greater clarity.

May you be thoroughly blessed, encouraged, built, and exhorted as you read these pages.

Chapter One

BLUEPRINT FOR LIFE

Is there a blueprint for life? For me, the answer is a resounding *yes!* And throughout this book I hope to convince you that my answer is correct. Many people think life is complicated and complex, full of challenges and difficulties. Therefore, they believe they must muddle through, creating their own way, according to their own belief system— hoping for the best. They carry on living the best life they can, eating, drinking, and being merry, because they don't know what might be coming their way!

Of course, life isn't always easy and it does frequently present us with great challenges. However, for those who believe in a gracious heavenly Father who is a good God and always eager to help, life can be very fruitful, full of adventure and excitement. When He is an integral part of our lives, **difficult** *circumstances can produce* **good** *fruit*—even trauma and disaster can be redeemed. Our magnificent God is able to bring good out of everything that we go through because of His great love for us.

God Loves You

God assures us of His love in many ways. For example, He speaks many wonderful and encouraging words to us in the pages of the Old Testament. But there is one Scripture passage in particular that should warm our hearts: "For I know the thoughts that I think toward You, says the Lord, thoughts of peace and not of evil, to give you a future and a hope. Then you will call upon Me and go and pray to Me, and I will listen to you, and you will seek Me and find Me, when you search for Me with all your heart" (Jer. 29:11-13).

Millions of people wrongly believe that God is harsh and far-away—an abstract Being who doesn't really care about them, and who certainly is not involved in their day-to-day life. Chances are, if you are reading this book, then you certainly do believe in God. It is my great joy and privilege to assure you that *He loves you* more than you could ever imagine. All of His thoughts toward you and about you are good!

FILLED WITH PEACE

According to the Scripture in Jeremiah, God's thoughts toward you are filled with peace. This is what He says about Himself as He reveals what He is like in His Word. God thinks about you always, you are forever on His heart. And His every thought about you is *filled with peace.* That means that He is *never upset* when He is thinking about you; neither is He *ever disturbed* in His thoughts about you. Each of His precious thoughts about you is full of deep and genuine heavenly peace. He cannot even think evil thoughts about you; it's impossible, because there is *no* darkness, *no* unkindness, *no* meanness, and *no* evil at all in Him on which to base such thoughts. *God is a good Father whose heart is full of love toward you!*

If you are a father or mother, you know that sometimes when you look at your children, you feel an overwhelming love for them. Even when they have done something wrong, you can't help yourself—you still love them. You can look at your children at night and just cry with love for them.

Well, if that is how you feel toward your children, how much more does God feel love toward His children. Those beautiful thoughts and that loving feeling that you experience come from Him. He is the source of that great, unconditional, self-sacrificing love.

As the verse in Jeremiah 29 says, not only does every thought toward you carry His *peace,* when He thinks of you He sees your future as well.

A Wonderful Future and Destiny

God has called us to be at His side and predestined us for a life with Him. He feels a great longing for our love and friendship, and loves to communicate and have intimate fellowship with us. In order to see that desire fulfilled, He has given us everything that we need for a life together with Him when He calls us. And He has also prepared good works in advance for us to do. All of our future is in His hands and He has a plan for each one of us.

It is also very encouraging to know that God has overwhelming *hope* for us as well. He can see us being with Him, and loving Him—enjoying His companionship as we work together to see His Kingdom established on the earth. In fact, since He is thinking about us constantly, His heart is always overflowing with *peace* and *hope* for the future He has planned for us. He can see us enjoying all our life together with Him as we move into the good future He has planned for each of us.

It's only when you understand something of the heart of God toward you that you can really begin to relax and rest knowing that He loves you, and that He has a great life and good things for you.

That's why He goes on to say, "Then you will seek Me and find Me...." If we don't know that He loves us, it's difficult to rest and from that place seek out His heart for us. We can really begin to rest and relax when we understand the heart of God toward us, knowing that He loves us and has a great life full of good things planned for our future. When we are not convinced of His love for us, it is impossible to be at rest and seek out His heart for us with confidence.

> **God loves you.**
> **Every thought He has about you**
> **is full of peace and hope.**
> **He has an exciting future planned for you.**

Not in Our Own Strength

As I unfold this blueprint that I believe that God has given us for life, it is important to remember that none of it can be carried out in our own strength. It is not something we can work out apart from the help of His Holy Spirit. Neither can we walk out His plans for us apart from His Word.

When I became a Christian, over 25 years ago, I knew that Jesus had visited me and performed an internal operation. Although I felt I had been given a whole new heart and life, I didn't really understand all that happened at that time.

As a boy, I had gone to church with my parents every week and had taken part in Bible studies and question times. I even made some money playing the piano and organ. I *liked* what I heard about Jesus very much. But I *did not like* the state of the church. At 14 years of age, church looked like a place full of miserable, sad, and depressed people. Jesus I liked, but I did not want to become like the people I saw attending church!

A NEW HEART

As I said, I didn't really know what had happened to me when Jesus visited me. I experienced a new and real love for people around me and began to think thoughts that I had never thought before. I saw things in a new way; even the flowers and the trees looked more green and beautiful.

I had heard about this Jesus who could save and transform people's lives—now it had happened to me. I couldn't deny it even though I didn't fully understand it, but I knew without a doubt that something powerful and life-transforming had taken place within me. Everyone around me knew it as well.

Eventually I understood it as well, and I saw it in God's Word, "I will give you a new heart and put a new spirit within you; I will take the heart of stone out of your flesh and give you a heart of flesh. I will put My Spirit within you and cause you to walk in My statutes, and you will keep My judgments and do them" (Ezek. 36:26-27). Jesus visited me and performed an internal operation in my heart and soul. I knew that this operation was the same as He had talked about with Nicodemus, a ruler and teacher of the Jews, all those years before when He walked upon the earth. He called it being born of the Spirit. (See John 3.)

AN INTERNAL OPERATION

When people believe upon the name of Jesus and all that He has done for them, they are saved and born again by His Spirit. At that moment, even though people may not understand what is happening within them, the Spirit of God comes upon them and begins to do a work within them. As we read in Ezekiel, in those moments the old stony heart that had been so hard and unfeeling, living only for itself, is removed, and we are given a heart transplant. The Father gives us a feeling heart—a heart that feels and is full of the love that He pours into our new heart: "because the love of God has been poured out in our hearts by the Holy Spirit who was given to us" (Rom. 5:5). At the same time He gives us this new heart, our inner being, or spirit self is also recreated; thus we have a new heart and a new spirit. In addition to all this, our heavenly Father puts His Spirit within us.

Everyone who has been born again has undergone this internal transformation whether he or she is aware of it or not. Although we cannot see the Spirit of God with our physical eyes, Jesus tells us about the things He will do within us. He will teach us about all things, lead and guide us, help and comfort us, and show us things to come. He will also strengthen us and deliver God's grace and abundant life. As believers, He lives within us, bringing all that He is to our lives and *He is God.*

Prior to this life transformation, many of us were *trying* to live a good life. Even though we instinctively knew right from wrong, good from evil, no matter how badly we wanted to do what was good, we inevitably failed. After we trusted in the finished work of Jesus, this internal operation took place, and we discovered that we were different. Everything became new. We had new thoughts, ideas, love, and understanding. Even our entrenched mindsets began to change as we learned about God's love for us and the ways of His Kingdom.

Just like the Scripture in Ezekiel says, when the Holy Spirit came to live on the inside, we began to "walk in His statutes." We began to walk in His way, empowered by His life inside us.

EMPOWERED BY HIS LIFE

What a relief it was to find that Jesus did a life-transforming work in me by His Spirit, enabling me to begin walking in a way that was pleasing to Him. I could now experience an intimate relationship with the Father who had always loved me and who had planned and purposed a wonderful life for me together with Himself. As His love was poured into my new heart, I was able to experience it flowing through me toward both God and others.

When I read or heard the Word, instead of trying to obey in my strength, I found His enabling power within me helping me. I was no longer alone, no longer living for myself. God the Father, Son, and Holy Spirit had found and called me—now They wanted to make Their home within me. The more I walked in the light of His truth, agreeing with God's thoughts, the more I found the Holy Spirit speaking to and blessing me—and the more of His life flowed through me to others.

> **God transforms and empowers your life with a new heart, spirit, and the Holy Spirit.**

REALIZATION

I quickly realized that if I wanted to experience the reality of His fullness in my life, I would have to cooperate with Him, allowing Him to teach me. Because I had experienced years and years of "doing my own thing," I had developed mindsets that had to be destroyed and replaced with His thoughts and ways. There were many times when I had to choose to submit my rebellious and stubborn will as I repented and received His grace. This is a process that I and all of those who are called by His name find themselves in. It is not always easy, and we do not always want to hear Him.

BY HIS SPIRIT

None of the things we have discussed so far can ever happen apart from His Holy Spirit and supernatural strength, the result of His life flowing through you. None of it—receiving a new heart, being empowered to transform into His image—could ever happen without a personal relationship with God who answers our continual cries for His help and life to change and sustain us.

As I have walked with Him over the years, I have come to understand that He loves me so much. He has an incredibly wonderful plan—a blueprint for my life. This is the case not just for my life, but for all those who want to find and enjoy life in the Kingdom, while still living upon the earth.

You can find your blueprint within the pages of the New Testament, and you can only see it as you are enlightened by the Holy Spirit. In fact, you can only act upon and obey God's blueprint by the power of the Holy Spirit within. As you are obedient to His Word, you begin to understand that there is a process, a way in which you can come into the fullness of His life. As you cooperate with this process, the Lord deals with your old attitudes and mindsets. These changes result in gaining a new perspective about the Kingdom of God. You begin to see what sort of Kingdom it is as well as see things about this world and how it operates.

As we follow His blueprint for our lives, we begin to experience His life and power more and more. It is important to keep in mind that Jesus says *it is not an easy way*. Rather the way to life is confined, narrow, and sometimes challenging—but in the end, it leads into real, authentic Christian *life*!

> *Then Jesus said to His disciples, "If anyone desires to come after Me, let him deny himself, and take up his cross, and follow after Me. For whoever desires to save his life will lose it, but whoever loses his life for My sake will find it"* (Matthew 16:24-25).

Chapter Two

JESUS, THE MASTER CRAFTSMAN

Whenever anyone is going to build, restructure, or reform something, they begin with a blueprint—a photographic copy of a plan. I believe that God never does anything without a plan. Whatever He is creating, designing, producing, bringing forth, He always has a plan and a purpose that is crystal clear. There is nothing that takes Him by surprise, nothing that shocks Him, nothing that He hasn't thought through, thought out, and thought about!

We read often throughout the Old Testament that things were built "according to the pattern" (see Exod. 25:40, Num. 8:4, Josh. 22:28, Heb. 8:5). There is nothing in the heart of the King or in His Kingdom that is not created or built without it being according to His pattern and His heart.

More important than anything that has ever been built upon the earth, the Father of all creation and everything that is and will be has a master plan for your life. That's because *you* and I are the most important creation upon the earth! Listen to what Jesus has to say about creation and the moment that humankind inhabited the earth.

> *Then I was beside Him as a master craftsman; and I was daily His delight, rejoicing always before Him, rejoicing in His inhabited world, and my delight was with the sons of men* (Proverbs 8:30-31).

This Scripture in Proverbs is found in the Old Testament. It is speaking specifically of the time of creation. Although here the Scripture is speaking of wisdom, we know from the New Testament that Jesus, the One and only beloved Son of the Father, is both the "power and the wisdom of God" (1 Cor. 1:24).

So I believe that this passage in Proverbs is about Jesus, the Word, at the very beginning. Here He is beside the Father as a Master Craftsman crafting the earth in perfect design. But even after He has done all these wonderful things, His delight is the "sons of men."

It's clear to me from this Scripture that although God created the world by speaking, "Then God said..." yet the Father, the Son (the Word), and the Holy Spirit had spent time thinking through every aspect of what would be and how They would do all that They had planned and purposed.

> **God had a blueprint for all that would take place the moment creation was spoken into being!**

God is both spontaneous and orderly (organized) at the same time. Although it appears to us as though He just "does it," He has in fact planned it, purposed it, and ordered it beautifully well beforehand.

Let's listen to Jesus some more:

The Lord possessed me at the beginning of His Way, before His works of old. I have been established from everlasting, from the beginning, before there was ever an earth. When there were no depths I was brought forth, when there were no fountains abounding with water. Before the mountains were settled, before the hills, I was brought forth; while as yet He had not made the earth or the fields, or the primal dust of the world. When He prepared the heavens, I was there, when He drew a circle on the face of the deep, when He established the clouds above, when He strengthened the fountains of the deep, when He assigned to the sea its limit, so that the waters would not transgress His command, when He marked out the foundations of the earth, then I was beside Him as a master craftsman... (Proverbs 8:22-30).

This shows us clearly that whenever God (the Father, Son, and Holy Spirit) does anything, it is always well thought through. It is architecturally sound. It is drawn and worked out. Wisdom always goes before and prepares everything in order so that it can be built and established as God desires.

JESUS AND HIS BLUEPRINT

If this is how it is with a solid mass, with a solid structure that has no "breath of God" within it, how much more so is it for us, whom He has chosen to be His adopted kids! Because God took so much care and attention to create the earth and made it so beautiful for us, how much more does He desire that our lives have a plan and a purpose? Jesus is the Master Craftsman of the earth and all that He has created—He is also the Master Craftsman of our lives. He has a blueprint by which we can become all that He has planned and purposed for us to become!

In the New Testament and the letter to the Corinthian church, the apostle Paul uses this same terminology to describe the function and gift that he had become to the church:

> *According to the grace of God which was given me, as a wise master craftsman I have laid the foundation, and another builds on it. But let each one take heed how he builds on it* (1 Corinthians 3:10).

God doesn't want us to muddle through life. He doesn't want us to be alone and without help. He has a plan and purpose for each one of us. And in the end, He wants us to look like Jesus in terms of our character and being. He wants us built with strong established foundations upon which He can build more and more through us, showing and making the life of Jesus manifest through us all together.

Therefore, He sent to us our Savior and redeemer Jesus Christ, His One and only beloved Son. He dealt with our sin, our iniquity, our transgressions, our infirmities, all our weaknesses and failings. He took the old and gave us the new—that we are new creations in Christ.

Jesus was also sent as the Apostle—the Master Craftsman—to build us into all that we can be and will be, by and through the power of His Holy

Spirit. This was always His plan—to build us and establish us in Him, both individually and even more importantly together as His Church.

> **God always uses a blueprint according to His plan.**
> **He builds from the foundation upward.**

THE MASTER CRAFTSMAN = THE APOSTLE

Jesus is the great Apostle, the sent One, the Master Craftsman who came to bring us the blueprint for our lives. The disciples, whom Jesus chose, became apostles, master craftsmen who would be able to build people's lives according to His plan. Paul was a master craftsman appointed and chosen by God.

And Jesus revealed that even as He ascended into Heaven, "He Himself gave some to be apostles, some prophets, some evangelists, some pastors and teachers" (Eph. 4:11).

FIVEFOLD MINISTRY

Why would Jesus reveal these ministries? Because His plan and intention is for the people of God to be built and established in Him to do the works of service and come into fullness.

By the time of Pentecost, 50 days after the death and resurrection of Jesus, the disciples were ready. Jesus had taught them, re-programmed them, re-tuned them, and finally they had been born again, which could only happen after His death and resurrection. Internally, everything was in order. They had been trained and discipled, they had become true sons of the Father, ready to prepare and train others, fathering them into the same spirit of sonship. All Father God had to do was add *power*. Internally they were ready; now they would receive a *clothing of power* that would fill them and fall on them, enabling them to be His witnesses.

When the Church was born on that day, power was supplied. What were needed were the people gifts and tools to *build* the Church according to the pattern that the Lord had purposed. These twelve men who were chosen to walk with Jesus and called to be apostles had now become those apostles—master craftsmen ready to build the church together according to the original blueprint that was in the heart of the Father.

Nothing Has Changed

This is still His plan. Nothing has changed. Until the Church grows up, until it comes to unity of the faith and begins to find fullness in Him, the apostolic and prophetic nature of the Church will continue and it will increase.

At the church here in Shipley, United Kingdom, I have been the one to build the church. I have laid the foundation of Christ in the hearts and lives of individual believers as well as in the church as a whole. This is the building gift that I am. Adam, a man whom I have discipled and trained, now pastors the church. This is the gift that he is and although he can read the pattern, he does not have the wisdom or anointing to build in this way—yet.

Without apostolic understanding and life, the blueprint for life will never come into fullness; it is already given, but without that ability to see, without the anointing that is needed to unfold it and build in like manner as the Master Craftsman, we individually and corporately will not come into fullness.

As best and as simply as possible, I want to try and unfold some of that blueprint to you. To do so, we may have to examine terminology that may be unfamiliar and outside your accepted Christian viewpoint. But let's remember that these words are the canon of Scripture. They are words that God Himself has chosen to use and that the Holy Spirit is completely at home with and understands fully. He is our Teacher and He will, in His grace, help us see and understand the truth of His own Word.

Apostle and the Depth of Its Meaning

What does it mean to be truly apostolic?

As already discussed, Jesus was and is the Apostle and High Priest of our confession. In Hebrews 3, we read that Moses was faithful in the house to which he was called. Jesus was also called to build a house—us. He is the Master Craftsman and He has the blueprint to build us correctly as a temple and house in which the Holy Spirit shall live and glorify God through us.

In order for anything to be built correctly and established properly, there must be a foundation.

We know that the foundation of our lives is Christ Jesus, "For no other foundation can anyone lay than that which is laid, which is Jesus Christ" (1 Cor. 3:11). This of course is the apostle Paul speaking of what he has been called to do through the grace of God—lay foundations.

FOUNDATIONS MUST BE LAID

So Jesus is our foundation. This foundation—Jesus—must be laid and built up in each believer's life. The reality of the truth must be built within each of us and then through us together.

> "...the Apostle and High Priest of our confession, Christ Jesus" (Hebrews 3:1).

This Apostle sacrificially gave up His life so that we might have life; He did this in, by, and through the power of the Holy Spirit. All the prophets and apostles both before and after Jesus were required to follow the example of Jesus. *Only when we live in this same manner can we build on the same foundation that He laid.*

The foundation of the Church is Christ Jesus, the One who in love sacrificially gave His life for all others.

If the Church is to be apostolic, it must be in both doctrine and life. A truly apostolic and prophetic church gives its life, in love, through and by the power of the Holy Spirit so that others may experience and have the life of God that flows through that offering.

Remember:

❖ God became a Man—Jesus Christ.

❖ That Man became a bond servant.

❖ That Bond Servant became an offering poured out.

❖ That Selfless Life poured out brought love, life, and power into earth's arena.

❖ That Life was multiplied and is to be reproduced throughout the earth.

That is truly what it means to be apostolic.

This book is the simple unfolding of the journey to living an apostolic life, the only one that provides the blueprint for our lives.

Chapter Three

REVOLUTION OF LOVE

Over the years, I have heard much teaching about the prophetic church. I believe that the church is to be prophetic in nature. Without the Lord speaking and revealing His heart and plans to the prophets, it is not possible to build the church correctly, and without the church partaking of that same nature, it is not possible for the church to impact and influence the world.

More recently I have been hearing about the apostolic church and what it is that makes the people of God apostolic and prophetic. Although there has been a lot of good revelation and teaching to help and encourage people, I have never heard what I truly believe makes a real, authentic people of God apostolic. *I believe that the true biblical foundation upon which any apostolic church must be built is the love of God demonstrated in laying down one's life.*

We see this apostolic foundation confirmed in the life of Jesus. In Hebrews 3 it says that Jesus, the One and only begotten Son of the Father, was also the great *Apostle and High Priest.* In an act of love, predestined from before the world began, He laid down His life for us (see Eph. 1:3-8). We also see this in the very nature of God Himself who sent His only Son to die on the cross.

DOMINION OF LOVE

As Christians we believe that the Bible is the Word of God—a love letter from Father God to His children. It expresses not only how He thinks and feels about us, but gives us insight into how things began, how they progressed, and how they will ultimately end. It also contains incredible revelation about a whole host of other things pertaining to life and godliness on an everyday basis. One of the key teachings of this incredible Book is found in First John 4:16, which tells us that *God is love...*

Because this clear declaration of His being is found in the Bible, we can believe and receive it in faith as an *absolute fact.* Because He is a loving God, He is truthful, faithful, and completely trustworthy. Apostle Paul confirms this fact of God's nature in writing to Titus when he refers to God *who cannot lie* (see Titus 1:2).

Therefore, if God is love, then the dominion of God is love. His Kingdom is filled with love and everything He does, all He touches, everywhere He is—is love. The big question: how does this love come to us? How do we personally know and experience God as love?

By This We Know

By this we know love, because He [Jesus] laid down His life for us... (1 John 3:16).

In the beginning, before the world was created, before the Word was spoken forth from the heart of the Father, the Father, Son, and Holy Spirit were together enjoying sweet communion and unbroken fellowship with one another. Distinct from each other, and yet One, they experienced oneness in all they thought, did, and spoke.

But because of God's nature of love, it was never enough that the three of them just enjoy themselves together. They wanted to enjoy everything with those who would be *sons and daughters* of the Father. In keeping with God's nature of total unselfish love, He wants to share everything that He is, everything that He has, and all He has done with His creation. God found a way to satisfy this desire of His heart by sending His Son to the cross. Now, our hearts are touched by His love when we know that He laid down His life for us.

When our hearts and lives are touched by God's love, the Kingdom of God invades and penetrates the earth further with power to save and change lives as we choose to live a selfless life. Conversely, the more selfish humankind becomes, the less the life and love of God is able to touch the hearts of men and women. *God's love is poured out into our hearts and, therefore, we can live and love like He does.*

CHOOSING OUR OWN WAY

The problem God faced was that He knew ultimately the men and women He created in His image would choose to exercise the free will He had given them by doing things their own way. Even though He had created them in love and breathed His life into them, He knew they would want to live for themselves. (There is a short chapter at the end of this book that discusses more thoroughly the subject of free will.)

Free will means that we can choose to walk away from His plan and purpose for our lives (see Jer. 29:11-13), and go our own way to do our own thing, "As it is written: *there is none righteous, no, not one; there is none who understands; there is none who seeks after God. They have all turned aside; they have together become unprofitable; there is none who does good, no, not one*" (Rom. 3:10-12).

Rather than choose a *selfless* way of life in the image of God, humankind would choose a *selfish* life characterized by decisions that pleased themselves. God could have predetermined that each and every one would love Him and live for Him. But in spite of the dire consequences, God chose not to override our will in order to "make" us believe. He would not abuse our right to choose, thus displaying again His great love for us.

A MASTER PLAN

Knowing that selfishness would be the tendency of humankind and being desperate to love us, God crafted a master plan. A blueprint for all He planned and intended. The Trinity—Father, Son, and Holy Spirit—made a way of escape from a life of selfishness for those who would choose it. Through those who choose this life, God purposed to touch the world. Together, they decided that the Son of the Father, Jesus, would come to earth and lay down His life, in every way, from conception to death on the cross; He would lay down His life completely. In giving His life away and surrendering everything at the cross, He would make a way for the love of God to penetrate the hearts of men and women as never before. At the same time, He would take away the sin of the whole world and all that stood between His loved ones and Himself.

> *By this we know love, because He* [Jesus] *laid down His life for us* (1 John 3:16a).

Giving your life for another is the number one principle in God's Kingdom of love. Following Jesus' ultimate and practical example of laying down His life for others, now, "we also ought to lay down our lives for the brethren" (see 1 John 1:16b).

> *Greater love has no one than this, than to lay down one's life for his friends* (John 15:13).

It is only as we lay down our lives, giving ourselves first in love to God and then to those around us, that we can begin to experience the real kind of God-life.

Principle #1 in God's Kingdom of love:
Give yourself sacrificially for others in love.

The number one principle in God's Kingdom of love is the giving of yourself selflessly and sacrificially for another in love. How do we live like this? Remember, "...the love of God has been poured out in our hearts by the Holy Spirit who was given to us" (Rom. 5:5). The blueprint for living life is established upon this very same principle, and is attained by allowing the Holy Spirit to live and walk through us by His love.

God, who is selfless, gives Himself continually so that we might have life. He is always for us, working for our best interest, never His own selfish purposes. In fact, nothing selfish can ever be part of His Kingdom. That is why when pride was found in the heart of that beautiful cherub and archangel, lucifer, who was created to praise and serve God, he was cast out of Heaven. "How you are fallen from heaven, O shining star, son of the morning! You have been thrown down to the earth..." (Isa. 14:12 NLT). There is no place in Heaven, the home of selfless love, found for lucifer and the wicked angels who chose to follow him in rebellion against the Lord.

INFINITE WISDOM

In their infinite wisdom, the Father, Son, and Holy Spirit decided that just as the selfless life of God ruled and reigned in His Kingdom, so it would invade and rule on the earth through the giving of Jesus' life on the cross. In this way, the life of God could flow among humankind in ever increasing measure. *Few have understood this wisdom of God's Kingdom and even fewer have chosen to live by giving their lives to the Father in such a way.*

Even Jesus' disciples who were the first to hear it, see it in action, and experience it for themselves, had trouble comprehending such love and had to be trained in this principle of life from death. In fact, at one point, Jesus rebuked Peter for not understanding this most important principle. In Matthew 16:21-27, Christ corrects Peter for his lack of understanding. When Jesus talked about His death on the cross, Peter said, "This shall not happen to you!"

Peter thought he knew better, that there was a better way of accomplishing God's will. He could not understand how this Man, Jesus, who had all power and authority—who could heal the sick, cast out demons, feed the multitudes, and even raise the dead—would have to go to Jerusalem to suffer and die! His thinking was full of the ways of the world. The enemy of God who had infiltrated the hearts and minds of people on earth, whispered these thoughts to Peter. That is why Jesus turned to Peter in Matthew 16:23 and said, "Get behind me, satan!"

Jesus went on to say, "If anyone desires to come after Me, let him deny himself and take up his cross and follow Me" (Matt. 16:24). In other words, we must humble ourselves and become like little children, giving up our own thinking, our own opinions, and our own way of doing things. Only in this way can we freely receive and know His love in our hearts and lay down our lives for others.

When we first came to know Jesus, we humbled ourselves. We gave up our own agendas and rights, we understood that we had been doing our own thing and walking in our own selfish way. As we humbled ourselves, He gave us the right to enter into the Kingdom of God. The Spirit of God came to us and began to work within us and upon us. Often, though, as we continue in our Christian pilgrimage, we take upon us a pride and selfishness that hinders His work within us.

ANOTHER KINGDOM

Although Peter didn't like it, or understand it, Jesus came from another Kingdom—*a Kingdom founded upon one never-ceasing, never-changing
fact that God is love.* And this love is expressed by the selfless laying down
of His life for us. His example is one that everyone who is born of God
must follow to experience the fullness of the life God intended.

God knew that the only way this love of the Kingdom could penetrate the ice-cold hearts of men was for Jesus to lay down His sinless
life on the cross. When Jesus gave Himself in this supreme act of loving, unprecedented power and authority from the Kingdom of God
was released upon the earth. The release of this power defeated satan
and all of God's enemies once and for all. *Having disarmed principalities
and powers, He made a public spectacle of them* [at the cross], *triumphing
over them in it* (see Col. 2:15).

It was the selfless love of Jesus Christ that totally and utterly defeated our enemies, disarming them, breaking chains of bondage, and
delivering humankind. Therefore, we can now choose to live in this
same love and see people set free as a result. Surely if the enemy had
known, he would "not have crucified the Lord of glory" (see 1 Cor. 2:8).

FOLLOWING HIS EXAMPLE

God knew that the only way for His love, power, grace, and authority
to flow upon the earth and into the hearts of men, women, boys, and
girls, was through the sacrificial giving up of His Son. No one would
ever be able to understand and experience Kingdom life until this
principle had been exemplified in Christ's life.

Even Peter and the disciples had to be dragged to the cross kicking
and screaming, because they were struggling to comprehend this and
give up their own ways, thoughts, and dreams. It wasn't until they actually saw the Lord crucified that they began to understand this life principle in the Kingdom of God.

> **All authentic life that touches humankind must first be
> laid down and die before it can be raised up in power!**

All real, genuine, authentic life that touches earth and humankind must first be laid down and die before it can be raised up in power. This sacrificial giving of life is the foundation that the household of God is built upon, "having been built on the foundation of the apostles and prophets, Jesus Christ Himself being the chief cornerstone" (Eph. 2:20). Jesus took His place as Chief Cornerstone because He laid down His life. When we come to Him, we are coming to One "...who is the living cornerstone of God's temple. He was rejected by people, but He was chosen by God for great honor. And you are living stones that God is building into His spiritual temple..." (1 Pet. 2:4-5 NLT).

So anyone who desires to live "according to the pattern" that Jesus laid down by His own life and gave as a blueprint for each of us, any desirous to be an apostolic people, or church built by the Master Craftsman, is one who not only believes the message of Christ crucified and risen again, but one who also *lives in that same heart attitude of being willing to lay down his or her life for others.*

Jesus laid down His life for us and that's how we know the love of God. When *we lay down our lives for others*, we become like Him, an example of the Father's love. It is from the foundation of this kind of love that the true authority and power of God is released on the earth.

Note: please understand that when I speak of "laying down of life" I am not only speaking in physical terms, but also as a mentality and lifestyle choice—laying down our lives in terms of time, effort, giving, hospitality, etc.

FULLNESS OF TIME

God never had any other way planned to establish His Kingdom on earth. This is the way it has been built since the beginning. The Old Testament prophets had to experience great difficulties, trials, and tribulations in order to enter into the Kingdom of God and have the Kingdom enter into them. *They had to embrace a lifestyle of death to self so that they might live.* As they embraced this lifestyle, they saw glimpses of the Kingdom of God on earth, but not the fullness.

But *when the fullness of time had come*, the Father sent His One and only begotten Son to give Himself up, laying down His life for us so that the Kingdom could burst forth in fullness upon the earth. The disciples who were called by Jesus to be apostles would also hear this message. They would see and experience it, eventually walking in the reality of it themselves. Then as they lay down their lives, it would be released through them into the lives of those who were looking to them as examples. *Embracing a lifestyle of death to self is required of everyone called to be an apostle.*

WHAT'S IN A NAME?

When Jesus talked about the foundation of apostles and prophets in the Church, He was introducing a new way of building His Kingdom on earth. Once when I was on a ministry trip, the Lord asked me, *"Why did I name them apostles?"* He wasn't asking me because He didn't know the answer, but because it was something He wanted me to think about. His answer had to do with the new model of leadership He introduced on the earth during His time here.

Before Christ, God's chosen people, Israel, functioned like a great family. They were divided into twelve tribes, each tribe eventually having a head and elders. The result of this was that by the time Jesus came on the scene, each city and town had a synagogue, which was led by an elder. Israel also had judges and kings. *In choosing disciples, some of whom were to become apostles, Jesus was introducing a whole new leadership concept and model.*

CALLED TO HIMSELF

Jesus did not call His disciples together and name them elders, as was the Old Testament norm. Rather, He chose certain men who would learn to become like Him, under His guidance and discipline, and called them disciples. They were first and foremost called not to a position, but to Him—not to a ministry, a leadership title or role, but to learn to live in an intimate relationship with Him. From among these men *He chose twelve and called them apostles* (see Luke 6:13). Although they were named apostles first, only with intense discipline, training, and equipping from the Lord would they become the real thing. This of course would take place through the ministry of the Word and the Spirit. Just as we read that Judas *became a traitor*, likewise these other men *became apostles* (see Luke 6:16).

Jesus was purposefully and clearly beginning to establish a whole new leadership concept. In His divine wisdom, which had been hidden away for long ages, He now revealed the Church and its leadership model. All that He would need initially to lead and fit the church together—which was also a whole new concept revealed in Matthew 16—were *apostles*.

This must have been not only terribly frightening to the enemies of God, but also bewildering to anyone who heard it for the first time. I am sure that when Jesus called these men out, they were overwhelmed with a sense of God's will and purpose. Not only were they filled with a sense of purpose for their lives, but also with excitement for the new thing that was happening on the earth. At the same time, they also had very little understanding of what that would mean. In fact, if they had really understood what it would mean for each one of them personally, they may have been less enthusiastic and responded with greater sobriety and even fear!

Of course, I don't know exactly what took place at that time. But I do know that Jesus, the Father, and Holy Spirit, in their divine wisdom and insight, not only saw the birth of the Church on Pentecost, but also how and who they would use to put the *living stones* in place (see 1 Pet. 2:5), and these people would be called *apostles*.

There is no doubt according to Jesus' own words that He Himself is building the Church, "…I will build My church, and the gates of Hades shall not prevail…" (Matt. 16:18). He is doing this by His Spirit, and they together—Spirit and the Word—are causing the foundation to be laid and the people of God to be equipped and set in place through the gifts of men and women that He has given into the Church.

Before we look at the many characteristics of an apostle, let's consider Ephesians 4:11-12, "And He Himself gave some to be apostles, some prophets, some evangelists, and some pastors and teachers, for the equipping of the saints for the work of ministry…"

GOD'S GIFTS TO THE CHURCH

Paul was the recipient of a great deal of revelation not previously made known (see Eph. 3:1-7). In Ephesians 4:16 he refers to the new leadership model that Jesus Himself put in place for the church—stating that apostles, prophets, teachers, etc., would be gifts to the church. Gifts from the Father, which were given in order to establish and bring the church into maturity in order to be released into the works God had previously ordained.

Why did Jesus not name the disciples as elders? Clearly He did not. Instead, it says He named them apostles. Much of this issue will be unfolded as you journey through the book. But it is clear that these disciples who became apostles would be the leaders of the newborn Church on and after the day of Pentecost.

Although the apostles would all be seen as elders, Jesus set them apart in apostolic ministry, showing forth clearly that apostolic ministry was to be very significant and carry with it authority and government within the Church body. (This would come from and be founded and established in the principle of life coming from death.)

We read that the Church was born in an explosion of power; and although Jesus ushered in a very significant new pattern of leadership, perhaps because of the unprecedented and incredible growth of the Church in many places, elders were set into ministry but the release and appointing of gift ministry took a lesser place. Thus, eventually, shepherds and pastors became the norm of the Church, as did elders, but nearly all the other ministries had to be received and released freshly through the course of history. It is a natural thing also that we tend to take what has been the norm rather than press forward into something that is new and perhaps not as easily accepted.

It was always the Father's plan and purpose that those whom He appointed as fivefold gift ministry would be given to the church to establish and bring it to maturity. But in the initial burst of rapid growth, they may have felt unable to press forward completely into the new concept of leadership that Jesus had introduced.

The Nature of Apostles and Prophets

The Kingdom of God was fully released upon the earth as a result of Jesus' choice to lay down His life to do the Father's will. In the same way, the apostles and prophets would choose to lay down their lives to bring forth the Kingdom—sharing in His death to bring forth His life. In this way, they positioned themselves to not only teach doctrine, but also to be a living example of it. When God sovereignly appointed and called forth these gifts, He put within them the ability for those who were called to give themselves for the Church. He never intended to only equip men and women who would teach about the Kingdom, but to call men and women who, by His grace, would chose to *give their lives for the Kingdom.*

In the process of laying down their lives, they are able to understand apostolic revelation, and in turn unfold it to the Church. Incredible and wide-reaching authority to do the works of God is released as this apostolic lifestyle is taught and lived out.

More Like Him

Sometimes we forget that church is not about a series of teachings and doctrines that we hold, but rather about a Person. The Person of Christ, the Living One in whom is all life. *We have come to His Person.*

Of course, we do have doctrine, too. But doctrine is essentially knowledge of being in Him. It's about His heart, how He sees and thinks about things, what He has done and is doing, and who He is and who we are in this world and in the age to come. A more in-depth discussion comes later about the "apostle's doctrine," which makes the canon of Scripture.

Apostolic ministry is about life from death—knowing the selfless One and becoming like Him. It is foundational ministry that should always connect us to Jesus, building us together into a spiritual house that is pleasing to Him. And it is *always* Christ centered.

It is my observation that much of what is taught in the church today does not focus on Christ as the center. It does not leave us thinking more about Jesus, but rather focuses us on ourselves and what we can do. It is often more about what God can do *for* us and how we can become self-sufficient using all He has given us. Believers are encouraged to become motivated to prosper and be successful in the building of their own little domains—whether that is our families, church families, ministries, or businesses. If we were to put God's plumb line against the current, popular message spoken of as Christianity, I am sure that we would find ourselves well off center, and in some cases even naked and exposed.

As Jesus is the Master Craftsman, He will at some point be walking around the building of our lives together measuring us with His own plumb line. The blueprint of life will be established and fulfilled according to His own word and the pattern that He has set before us. The church here in Shipley has a number of new fledgling business ventures, the inspiration for which came out of a scripturally sound teaching forum specifically geared toward business. We are watchful to build business according to God's principles. We look at such foundational things as: seeking the Kingdom first, working to learn, the least of all—finance, eternal perspectives, faith—the currency of the Kingdom, honoring Him in everything, getting wisdom, plus much more. These principles are keeping us Christ-centered.

That is why the apostolic messengers and the incredible message they carry must be made known. If the church is going to become like Christ and be built into a beautiful temple in which He can dwell, it must be placed on this solid and firm foundation in order to stand.

There are many within the church today who teach that the ministry gifts of apostle, prophet, teacher, pastor, and evangelist are no longer relevant. They say that the only true apostles were those who had seen Jesus, who had been with Him, and who had experienced the resurrection of Christ. However, it is clear that Paul, as possibly the greatest apostle who was among those who did not see and spend time with Jesus, unlike the original twelve apostles, writes in Ephesians 4:16 that, these gifts will be *needed* and *remain until we (the church) reach a perfect and mature man...* I think we could all agree that the church is not yet perfect and mature; therefore these gifts must remain. Not at my say so, but at the Word of the Lord. Perhaps we would do well to learn how to humbly receive from, and gratefully look after, these precious gifts that God has given for the maturing of His Body, the Church.

To summarize, the godhead has a master plan, a blueprint for life. To bring this blueprint into the earth, the Father sent the Master Craftsman, Jesus the great Apostle. He was the One sent to build the church. The twelve disciples were called apostles, not elders, because they, like Jesus, would become master craftsmen called to put the living stones in place. Apostles are needed today to establish the Church and bring it to maturity.

Chapter Four

RECEIVERS AND RESPONDERS

Having looked at the true nature of God and His Kingdom, you have seen that the Father, Son, and Holy Ghost (Three in One) share a selfless nature. Everything they are and all they do come from a place of selflessness. They delight in sharing everything with one another and with Their creation.

In order to satisfy Their desire to share all that They are, They have brought to birth many children, offspring that They desire would love them of their own free will: children who are eager to cooperate in the process of growing into true sons and daughters of God who exhibit His same selfless nature. Remember as well that this selfless nature is the nature of God, and it flows from the love of God that is already poured out within us by His Spirit. As receivers of Their love and selfless nature, we need to be grateful responders.

According to chapter 1 of the epistle written to the church at Ephesus, Paul says that God the Father "chose us in Him before the foundation of the world, that we should be holy and without blame before Him in love, having predestined us to adoption as sons by Jesus Christ to Himself, according to the good pleasure of His will..." (Eph. 1:4-5).

Before the world, before Adam and Eve, before the Fall, God had already decided and purposed that through His Son we would be adopted as sons and become as His Son. This was the master plan, all written in the blueprint, and would be established and fulfilled through the great Apostle and Master Builder, Jesus Christ.

Indeed the Scripture tells us that through, *great and precious promises...we may be partakers of the divine nature...* (see 2 Pet. 1). This means that we, too, can learn to live sacrificially, with a giving, generous, and selfless nature like God's, motivated and sustained by love.

DRAMATIC INVASION OF LOVE

We have seen that Jesus, the only beloved Son of the Father, was also the great Apostle. Together with the Father and Holy Spirit, He decided that He would lay down His life for us (see First John 3:16). In this way, He set an example for us by demonstrating God's amazing, selfless love at the cross. Jesus' decision to love humankind unselfishly resulted in a pervasive and dramatic invasion of the Kingdom of God into our corrupt and desperately selfish world.

> **Jesus' decision to love humankind unselfishly resulted in a pervasive and dramatic invasion of the Kingdom of God into our corrupt and desperately selfish world.**

From my observations—hopefully I am mistaken—it seems that much of what is called Christianity in the church today has lost its solid foundation in the love of God. True, real love is not always a "nice feeling," although it can be that as well, but true love as seen in Jesus is the actual sacrificial and costly giving of one's own life for others, motivated by God's own Spirit and heart. Contrary to that, we often see the selfishness of the world infiltrating the church and the hearts of believers. Even though we are saved from sin, the selfish motivation to continue in it remains. We are consumed with finding ways to better and empower ourselves, and generally live a more "successful" life. Our focus is on ourselves, and our goal is to experience greater prosperity as we seek to fulfill our potential.

I know that God wants to see His children blessed and prospering. However, if our desire for His will in our lives is rooted in selfish, me-centered motivation, then we are not living according to the truth of the gospel. Those who have been saved have been given a new heart with new motivation. We now have the love of God in us and, like Him, we should no longer be living for ourselves, but for Jesus and His Kingdom, a Kingdom driven by love for God and others.

A FIRM FOUNDATION

As mentioned previously, in giving His life, Jesus became the Chief Cornerstone of the Church and its very foundation. As the great Apostle and Master Craftsman, Jesus has shown us by example that *the Kingdom is about selfless living and giving.* All who want to take their place as *living stones* in the Body of Christ must build their lives on this same foundation of selfless love. This is what true apostolic Christianity is really all about.

The gospel preached by the original apostles is that Christ lived, He died, and He rose from the dead for the sake of humankind. Christ Jesus' motivation for coming to live on earth, for dying on a cross, and for rising again was love. *This is what I term apostolic Christianity, a lifestyle motivated by love like that of Jesus.* This is a truth that I believe must be reemphasized and reestablished as the foundation of the church.

Therefore, everything that I am sharing has its source and principles in the selfless nature and character of God. When I talk about apostolic love, I am emphasizing the fact that to love in this way, you must *first* give up your own life and personal motivations. Only then can you partake of His life—real life that generates and motivates you to fulfill *His* purpose and plan on the earth. A true apostolic church will exemplify and live this kind of Christianity. An apostolic church is not just one that has apostolic oversight or apostles who speak into it; *it is a church that lives the apostolic life and message.*

> **An apostolic church is not just one that has apostolic oversight or apostles who speak into it; it is a church that lives the apostolic life and message.**

In terms of the blueprint for our lives, both individually and corporately, this must be built on the foundation which is already laid— Christ. This foundation is made of real love that gives itself for another selflessly.

Jesus gave His life to become our foundation; those who lay this foundation in the lives of others must also live in this same manner of life, empowered by His Spirit. As they build in this same life and love, those who partake of this ministry are also changed by it. Not only are they established on the solid foundation, but they begin to carry this same life to others around them. They receive and others respond.

The Nature and Character of the Church

We have looked at the incredible love of God toward the Church. That is the selfless, giving, sacrificial love of God that was demonstrated through His Son laying down His life for us. This kind of life is meant to be the foundation of *everything* in the Kingdom of God and first appeared on earth when Jesus was born in Bethlehem. From that time there has been a continual infusion of God's love on the earth, until the day Jerusalem experienced a powerful explosion of life at Pentecost. Life so full of God Himself that it penetrated this dark, depressed earth with its heavenly light, and it's now meant to continue being expressed through Christ's Body on the earth.

All the apostles whom Jesus called built further on this foundation as they followed His example, giving up their lives for the sake of His Kingdom. This is what I mean when I say that the nature of the real Church is apostolic; and this is the nature and character of the Church that is intended to become His Bride.

Bridal Love

I have often spoken from Ephesians 5 while conducting marriage ceremonies. Although it appears that this passage is about marriage, it actually has more to do with Jesus and the Church. As Paul says in verse 32, "This is a great mystery, but I speak concerning Christ and the church." Let's look at this passage in the light of how the Church is meant to respond to Jesus as a Bride.

Let's look at these verses from The Message Bible as we consider how much Jesus loves us.

> *Husbands, go all out in your love for your wives, exactly as Christ did for the church—a love marked by giving, not getting. Christ's*

love makes the church whole. His words evoke her beauty. Every-
thing he does and says is designed to bring the best out of her,
dressing her in dazzling white silk, radiant with holiness. And that
is how husbands ought to love their wives.... No one abuses his
own body, does he? No, he feeds and pampers it. That's how Christ
treats us, the church, since we are part of His body (Ephesians
5:25-29 MSG).

This not only shows us how a husband is to love his wife, but also
paints a picture of how Christ loves us. *Jesus loves us in such an amazing*
way! First, He gave Himself for us and took all our sin, pain, hurt, grief,
and sorrow unto Himself. At the same time, He washes, cleanses, and
prepares us; setting us apart, equipping us, and giving us all we need.
Everything He does is designed to give us security, identity, and purpose. *There's no holding Him back in making us right and releasing us into*
every good and wonderful thing that He has for us.

Christ's love for Mary Magdalene is a good example of Him walking
out the things we see in Ephesians. The following is a list of the fruits
of Jesus' love toward us as seen in her life. Keep in mind that this is the
way Jesus loves everyone whose life He touches.

Jesus freely loved Mary Magdalene in a way that:

❖ Gave her respect.

❖ Restored her beauty.

❖ Secured her in His love.

❖ Brought her to wholeness.

❖ Did not judge her.

❖ Gave her life and built her up internally.

❖ Made her feel like a new bride instead of dirty and unworthy.

❖ Covered her in beautiful garments of righteousness, making her radiant.

This is what Jesus did for Mary Magdalene and this is what He has
done for you. How will you respond to such amazing love?

LOVING MUCH

In Luke 7, Jesus says to Simon, "Do you see this woman? I came to your home; you provided no water for my feet, but she rained tears on my feet and dried them with her hair. You gave me no greeting, but from the time I arrived she hasn't quit kissing my feet. You provided nothing for freshening up, but she has soothed my feet with perfume. Impressive, isn't it? She was forgiven many, many sins, and so she is very, very grateful. If the forgiveness is minimal, the gratitude is minimal" (Luke 7:43 MSG).

We see here two very different people responding to Jesus' presence in two very different ways. Mary, who loved much because she was aware of what a sinner she was, experienced conviction in her heart in Jesus' presence. Her response was to give Him everything; she could do nothing less. Simon, who loved little because he was not aware of his sin, felt that he was all right in Jesus' presence and was content not to give Him even the normal considerations of a guest.

On the other hand, Simon had no trouble perceiving Mary's sin. In fact, everyone could see her sin. They all knew who she was and what she had done. It was about as external as sin gets! But Simon's sin, just as grievous, if not more so, was hidden, internal sin. He kept up good appearances and maintained an air of righteousness.

But which was worse?

Simon's condition:

- ❖ He was dirty on the inside.

- ❖ He judged Mary for her sin.

- ❖ He judged Jesus for His reaction to Mary.

- ❖ He was upset, critical, joyless, and took offence.

- ❖ He may not have used his body in the same way Mary had, but he had most certainly stored up rubbish in his mind.

This story relates to us because we, like Simon and Mary, are all sinners, "For all have sinned and fall short of the glory of God" (Rom. 3:23). Apart from Jesus, you and I would be tormented forever with the misery of our own failure, weaknesses, and sins. Our own darkness would torment and steal from us; our own judgments would imprison us. We don't need the devil to experience torment. The only way to really be free is to know the love of Jesus.

JESUS AS A LOVER

For all her wrongs and sins, when Jesus expressed His incredible, redeeming love to Mary, she responded to Him as a lover. All that she had learned in terms of expressing love externally (but now in a pure way), she put into practice, allowing the love inside her to be expressed externally.

Mary Magdalene was like the prodigal son who, when he saw his father running toward him with outstretched hands, responded by freely receiving his love and forgiveness. At the same time he acknowledged his sin, he received love and forgiveness from his father and therefore was able to give himself fully to him. No hindrances could stop them from rejoicing in their love for one another: father and son partied, loved, blessed, honored, danced, sang, and celebrated, *enjoying one another completely!*

But the older son was more like Simon. Even though he had all the same blessings as his brother, he was unable to rejoice with them at the party. No doubt when he looked at his brother, his thoughts were something like: *He's been to the brothel, he's wasted his inheritance on foolish things, and he's lived like a sinner. He is not worthy of our father's blessings.*

What he didn't realize was that in the very same breath, he became as much of a sinner as the brother he was so busy criticizing. So, now, he needed the same love and forgiveness from his father that upset him when his brother received it! The older brother was now imprisoned by his own sin that judgment, criticism, harshness, and bitterness became his jailers. He, too, would have to do what was right to become a free man. Like his younger brother, he would have to repent and receive the love and forgiveness of his father.

It wouldn't be enough for the older brother to simply say, "I'm sorry." He would have to join the party! Have you ever done this sort of thing on a Sunday morning? You come into a meeting and don't feel like worshiping God. Then you hear someone say something that encourages you to join in the praises. You respond with, "Yes, Lord I want to praise You, please forgive me." Only instead of joining in the "party" you go right back to the way you were before. That is not true repentance. That's just a half-hearted attempt to make yourself feel better. Repentance is only real when we change as a result. *If it doesn't lead you to salvation in terms of greater wholeness and life, then it is not real repentance.*

RADICAL LOVE

In contrast, Mary Magdalene had experienced real repentance leading to life, wholeness, and intimacy with Jesus.

Maybe Mary was meant to take the place of Judas as the twelfth apostle? She certainly met the criteria. There were, in fact, a number of women who followed Jesus. This was radical for them to do at that time. Think about it, even today a group of women devoting themselves to following a man like this would be considered radical, and even cultish.

In Mark 6:3 Scripture tells us that Jesus' mother and sisters were among the women who followed Him, "Is this not the carpenter, the son of Mary and the brother of James, Joses, Judas and Simon? And are not his sisters here with us?" In Luke 8:2-3 it also names several other women who followed Jesus, "And certain women who had been healed of evil spirits and infirmities, Mary called Magdalene, out of whom had come seven demons, and Joanna the wife of Chuza, Herod's steward, and Susanna, and many *others who provided for Him from their substance.*"

Among these women some were named specifically: some were married, some were family, and some were grateful followers who had been delivered from various problems.

In those days, women were generally "kept" for very basic although important reasons. They were expected to bear and raise children, work at home, look after their husbands, and whatever else was necessary to care for the family (a role that has been seen very negatively throughout much of history). They lived in the background of things, having very little influence, prestige, or status. Although their commitment to following Jesus may have made these women unusual, it did not stop them from living out their love for the Lord. The Bible leaves us with no doubt about how much they loved Jesus. Not only did they physically accompany Him from place to place, but they also honored Him by providing what He needed from their substance.

Whatever these ladies' particular status or "none" status in life, they had obviously met and fallen in love with the Lord of life! They gave up everything to follow Him; providing for Him in both life and death.

LOVE TRIUMPHS

When you have given up everything, it becomes much easier to perceive and understand the Kingdom of God. Among those close to Jesus, I find it very possible that only Mary Magdalene, who had given up everything, really understood what the Kingdom was all about. Jesus Himself says of her after she anointed Him, "Let her alone, she has kept this for the day of My burial" (John 12:7). Is it possible that she alone understood that Jesus would have to die for all of our sins? This, to me, is what Jesus seems to be saying.

She certainly behaved different from the men who were following the Lord. When He was crucified, all the men, with the exception of John, ran away. We find the record in Mark 14:50, "Then they all forsook Him and fled." Their visions of grandeur, their dreams of victory over Rome, and their hopes of greatness had all vanished at the cross. The words and promises of Jesus no longer seemed valid to them. Their conviction that Israel would become a kingdom once again, as in the days of David, disappeared. Only when they came face to face with the reality of the cross—and understood its significance—could their dreams and visions be raised again.

With the exception of the apostle John, the women stayed at the cross and suffered with Him through it all, "Now there stood by the cross of Jesus His mother Mary, and His mother's sister, Mary the wife of Clopas, and Mary Magdalene" (John 19:25). They refused to abandon Him in life, or in death! *The depth of their love triumphed over the strength of their fear.* Their love for Jesus was greater than any personal grief, sense of loss or failure that they were experiencing.

Because they had already given everything, they had nothing to lose and no reason to run away. It's not that they didn't have any desires or dreams that perished at the cross; they may have had all sorts of ideas for ministries they could start, or ways to minister to Jesus personally. But their love for Him was greater than their fears or doubts about the future.

After Jesus had been crucified and placed in the tomb, we find Mary Magdalene, Mary the mother of James, Joanna and several other women, right there with Him once again (see Luke 24:10). Truly apostolic love was at work in them, and I believe that true apostolic love can be seen throughout their lives. When they met Jesus, their whole lives were centered on His life, and eventually His death.

> **The depth of their love for Jesus triumphed over the strength of their fear and personal grief.**

A LOVER'S RESPONSE

In response to Jesus' love for her, Mary Magdalene shows us how we can love Him back—how we can bless, honor, and express our love to Him. When Jesus rebuilt her from the inside out, He poured His love into her and forgave her sin. He washed her, cleansed her, and gave her a whole new life; she responded by falling in love with Him. This was not some kind of clinical, religious, dry love; this was the love of someone who had fallen in love; someone who was a "lover" to Him. She understood that He had to lay down His life fully, that she might receive His life fully. That is why Jesus declared that what she had done would be spoken about for ages to come, in Heaven and on earth—so that we can learn from her example of *selfless, abandoned, passionate, sacrificial love for Jesus.*

Christ's love flowed to her, through her, and back again to Him—it was reciprocated. This is the love of an apostolic church for Jesus, the One who gave Himself for us. It is love that is not focused on us, our ministries, our dreams, our visions, or our possible prosperity, success, or gain. It is an all-consuming love that is totally taken up with responding to Him in love and loving His Body, the Church. When we respond to Jesus with this kind of love, we will enter new realms of freedom and liberty as we fulfill our destiny.

That is the Kingdom message; that's the love of God in the heart's of His people, given back to Him apostolic love from an apostolic church. That love is the solid foundation upon which Jesus can build our lives and see His master plan come to fruition. The blueprint has a foundation; now it needs directives to see it come to fullness.

Chapter Five

IMPLEMENTING THE BLUEPRINT

The apostles were normal men, men who were personally called and appointed by Jesus. They were trained in His training school, disciplined, equipped, and sent out on assignments to wherever the Father directed.

The men and women who walked with Jesus when He was on the earth were just like all the other men and women around at that time. The difference was that they became all that they could—all that God intended for them. The reason they realized all God had for them was because they had hearts hungry for something more. They recognized the Messiah, received His Word gladly, and chose to follow after Him not just one day, but every day.

I believe they were able to develop their full potential because they spent so much time with Jesus, watching and listening to Him. Regardless of their own failings and weaknesses and the opposition they experienced as a result of their choice, they committed to serving and walking with this God-Man who was making the things of God, theology, alive to them.

They saw and heard a Man who was empowered in a very special and unique way by the Holy Spirit, and yet this Man was also laying down His life continually and constantly for all those around. Their theology was founded on His attitude of love and sacrifice; this is where the *apostles doctrine,* now the canon of New Testament Scripture, came from.

ALL ABOUT JESUS

They knew Him personally, and as He spoke to them He unfolded things about faith, the Father, the Kingdom, and many other things pertaining to life. *So, for the apostles, theology was all about a Person, the Person of Christ.* Everything was centered on Him and His Father. Theology to them was not a cold study of facts. Neither was it information to be remembered. It was equated with Jesus and His Kingdom; everything revolved around Him. As He spoke, their minds were lifted into another realm; they could see the reality of it and learn from Jesus how to draw it down into the present where they lived.

Later, after Jesus had ascended to Heaven, I have no doubt that the apostles were completely taken up with Him as they were speaking to the believers who gathered. I'm sure that they spent time recalling the stories, reliving lessons, and rehearsing incredible events that they were privileged to witness. And as they spent time talking with the Lord in prayer, thinking about all He had done and said, and remembering the life He lived, they began to see greater things and unfold deeper revelation to those around them. We know this because we have the Gospel accounts that were written after His death and resurrection.

It says of the first church that, *they continued steadfastly in the apostle's doctrine and fellowship, in the breaking of bread, and in prayers....* They didn't do this because they were *forced* to do it. *They had all fallen in love with the Lord of life, and they did it because they could do no other.* They didn't have to make people meet together to pray, or to break bread, or to be taught. They *gladly* did these things. These disciplines were a normal outworking of their daily lives with Jesus and one another. Without these disciplines and directives it would not be possible to finish building; the blueprint would not be fulfilled.

MORE OF HIM

Everything the apostles taught was based in and upon Jesus. When they talked about success in life, they were thinking about *Kingdom life.* When they talked about prosperity and having more than enough, it was all *found in Him.* Of course, all this teaching was very motivational and inspiring, but at its core there was always a *Person.* And that's what apostolic teaching is like, it's founded and established in Christ. When you come away from it, you should know that you have seen something more of Him, more of His Kingdom, and more of His Father's heart.

As *His* love, *His* life, and *His* teaching affect your heart and mind, you begin to change and be transformed as well, not just to be a better person, but rather to be more of a Jesus person, more of a Kingdom person.

Apostolic doctrine is more about Him than it is about you. It's about what *He* says, what *He* has done, what *He* desires you to become, what *He* has planned, and what life is all about from *His* perspective, not yours.

Of course, the early disciples could never really fully understand Kingdom life and reality until after the death and resurrection of Christ; because it was there, at the cross, that the Father showed us His great, sacrificial love—the kind of love that He is, has, and always will be. That was the last and the greatest lesson about the Kingdom, that the love of God gives itself up for us all the time. *He lays down His life that we might have life—life comes from death.*

That truly is the kernel, the core, the heart of Christianity, because that truly is the heart of God. The Father, the Son, and the Holy Spirit live life in this way. That's why the apostle Paul says, "For Christ did not send me to baptize, but to preach the gospel, not with words of wisdom, lest the cross of Christ should be made of no effect. For the message of the cross is foolishness to those who are perishing, but to us who are being saved it is the power of God...For Jews request a sign, and Greeks seek after wisdom; but we preach Christ crucified...Christ the power of God and the wisdom of God" (1 Cor. 1:17-24).

All the teaching that Paul would do, and all the revelation he would receive and share with others, was founded and based in the cross of Christ—in the love of God and the work of His Son, the greatest Master Craftsman.

CRAFTSMEN NEEDED

Some Christians today have a problem believing that God still has a legitimate apostolic ministry on the earth. That attitude is the reason why so many churches are not built properly. Without apostolic ministry, the church and individuals who make up the church cannot be built properly or truly experience the fullness of His life according to the blueprint (or the pattern). We want to live a full life and our "best life now," but we will never truly be satisfied because we are not seeing the fullness of the plan. We know that the gifts of God are sovereignly given in order to bring the believers to maturity, unity, and godly order. These gifts are desperately needed in the church today. Craftsmen and women are needed. It is their hour; and in order to impart all God has given them for the church, they must be received and treated as the gifts from Heaven they are intended to be.

> **The gifts of God are sovereignly given to bring believers to maturity, unity, and godly order.**

It can't just be "any craftsman"; it must be a master craftsman according to the definition in the Word—in the likeness of Jesus and Paul. Otherwise we may have a great kitchen, but the rest of the house will be a mess!

Many pastors and teachers understand the pattern given because they can read it, but they do not have either the authority or the grace to bring the pattern into the fullness of life. Just as I mentioned in an earlier chapter, Adam is the pastor of Christian Life Church in Shipley. He can read the pattern, but does not yet have the specific wisdom or gifting needed to set everything in order or build it in the correct way. It's not enough to read and understand it. It's not enough to want it. God has ordered things in such a way that we need one another. Gift ministries need each other, and the Church needs all the God-given gifts it can get to grow into a state of maturity and order. Yes all the gift ministries are part of equipping and discipling believers, but the apostolic ministry is the one that sets everything in order and builds it all on the correct foundation.

BORN OUT OF TIME

Paul was not one of the twelve. He may have seen Jesus and possibly even heard Him speak, but he was not one of the twelve apostles of the Lamb. He was one born "out of time," one of those apostles who came after the first twelve. Of course, the first twelve were special in the sense that they were with Jesus as He walked and talked. They witnessed all

He said and did and gave testimony to that fact; but the case for those who struggle with apostles after Jesus, is lost with the fact that Paul was born out of season, *after* the twelve.

The evidence increases in strength as many are named apostles in the last chapter of the Book to the Romans. And there is much evidence in the first few centuries of Christianity that apostles were alive and thriving. In terms of Scripture, it is very clear, "And He [Jesus] Himself gave some to be apostles, some prophets, some evangelists, and some pastors and teachers for the equipping of the saints, for the work of ministry, for the edifying of the body of Christ *until* we all come to the unity of the faith and to the knowledge of the Son of God, to a mature man, to the measure of the stature of the fullness of Christ" (Eph. 4:11-13).

From our present perspective, Paul is seen as perhaps the greatest of all the apostles. He was most certainly a great master craftsman. But at the time he lived, he was probably not the flavor of the week—not even of the year! At that time, many people who now call him the greatest would have been challenged and found it difficult doing even a small percentage of what he sometimes "commanded" the leaders and churches to do in his time. Much of Paul's revelation and teaching was misunderstood; even Peter in his second epistle makes it clear that some were "twisting" Paul's words to their own destruction and that some of what he taught was not easy to understand. (See Second Peter 3:14-16.)

There is no doubt that Paul heard all the stories about Jesus. He was a disciple of Gamaiel, *brought up at his feet, and taught according to the strictness of our father's law,* before the Lord revealed himself to Paul (who was then Saul). He would have heard both good and bad, positive and negative reports about Jesus.

But Paul had a revelation of Jesus; he met the risen Lord in all His glory and power. So great was the brightness of His presence that Paul was blinded for three days. He heard the voice of the Lord speaking with him, and the word of the Lord was seeded into him at such a depth it changed his life immediately and forever. *He was never the same.*

The Spirit and the Flesh

From that moment on, Paul was a man of the Spirit and the Word. Talking to the Corinthian church, Paul exhorted the believers, "From now on we regard no one according to the flesh. Even though we have known Christ according to the flesh, yet now we know Him thus no longer. Therefore if anyone is in Christ, he is a new creation; old things have passed away; behold all things have become new" (2 Cor. 5:16-17).

Many in those days would have seen and heard Jesus "in the flesh." They would have known Him and thought of Him in the gospel kind of way: as the Man who walked on water; the Man who fed the five thousand; the One who performed miracles and healings; the One who had authority to deliver all manner of persons around Him from oppression. Much of the preaching and teaching that they heard would have been in this vain.

However, Paul taught through revelation by the Spirit. He was hearing and seeing in his spirit while being empowered by the Holy Spirit. He was searching out the deep things of God and making them known. Indeed, Paul brought forth mysteries—things hidden away for ages gone by in the heart and mind of God, which were revealed to his inner man, into his spirit, and then declared as truth, "Then after fourteen years I went up again to Jerusalem with Barnabas, and also took Titus with me. And I went up by revelation and communicated to them that gospel which I preached among the Gentiles..." (Gal. 2:1-2). Paul was moved by revelation that He received from God and that was the basis of all his teaching.

Paul was a most amazing man. Although he received deep revelation from the heart of God and brought forth mysteries, he never became exclusive or isolated from other believers. He continued to teach in the synagogues; and when they no longer would hear him, he found others who would gladly receive the word he had to bring.

In Christ

Paul and Barnabas went to Antioch, and for one whole year and, "...they assembled the church and taught a great many people. And the disciples were first called Christians in Antioch" (Acts 11:26). It was in Antioch where Paul brought forth the revelation of what it means to be "in Christ," or a Christian. Of course Jesus Himself had disciples— men and women He trained to be like Him and do what He did. But in the end, they were to be "in Him"—not just following Him or discipled by Him. So this is the doctrine that Paul brought forth; He taught the importance of being "in Christ." He writes much about us being "in Him" and Him being in us.

Paul was revealing the New Covenant, or New Testament. He expounded on the truth that Jesus had fulfilled the Old and brought forth the New. In His work on earth, Jesus had lined up everything for the New Covenant to become reality in the lives of those who loved and followed after Him. Paul was breaking open that new covenant, illuminating for men and women what had been made available in terms of what belonged to us, what we could expect, etc. All of which was *founded in* Christ and *available through* Him.

Old Verses New

In Jerusalem, Peter, James, and John had apostolic oversight for the Church. They had thousands to look after, including a large number of priests (those who administered the things of God in the temple and toward the people) who also had been saved. (See Acts 6:7.) Many of these became known as the circumcision, because they expected all who believed to not only be circumcised, but also do other things in keeping with the Law.

Even though the Old Covenant had been fulfilled by Jesus and the New brought in those who had lived in the old had massive problems changing their minds about some of the old things. Their hearts were new and they had been born again, but their *minds* were in a process of change—they found it hard to adjust and get in line with the new. Consequently, when anyone became a Christian they expected them to live by the rules, regulations, and stipulations of the Old Covenant. This caused no end of problems, not just in Jerusalem, but also in regions beyond where the Church was being established.

Paul fought hard for the truth to prevail. He hated religion in the sense of regulations and rules. He hated hypocrisy. In Galatians 2 he rebuked Peter and James for their hypocrisy when they stopped eating and fellowshipping with Gentiles because other Jews were present. Even though Christ had died to fulfill the Old Testament and instituted a wholly New Testament between Himself and His Father (in which we are made one), many still continued to live in the old ways.

A CONTINUING STRUGGLE

The same struggle between the old and the new continues today. In spite of the fact that we "say" we believe the new, we tend to cling to the old and resist significant change, even when God has sent us a Master Craftsman with knowledge from Heaven to lay the right foundation.

Paul was a master craftsman who had been given wisdom and grace from God to build the Church according to God's pattern and order. The plumb line was the Word of the Lord. Jesus Himself was the Chief Cornerstone, and the foundation, but others would lay (into the lives of the believers) this living foundation upon which the Church could be built. The New Covenant would be the present, legally binding testament upon which Jesus would establish His Kingdom on the earth. (In Chapter 16, you can read and then write your own name into The Testament—The Will of Jesus.)

> **Apostolic doctrine brings reformation.**

Apostolic doctrine brings reformation. Refreshing and revival are wonderful things, and we must believe that times of refreshing will be continually released among us. *However, what we so desperately need is not revival, but reformation.* The last great reformation was in Martin Luther's day, when a revelation of grace was brought forth along with other truths, which changed the Church forever. I believe that we are in a historical time when we need a similar reformation. *We need to not only **understand** the New Covenant, but we also need to **live in it** as though it really is ours!*

A NEW MINDSET

Much of the Church lives in immaturity because it refuses to leave the sinner mentality behind. It believes that somehow in order to remain humble and please God, we have to maintain an "I'm a miserable sinner attitude." That our "humility" will appease Him in some way. Many believers are trapped in the sin conscious mentality and have no idea about the righteousness of God mentality. Of course if we do not accept and submit to what Jesus has done for us, then we are both disobedient and dishonoring to Him! He really cannot do any more for us—it has been finished completely and totally. When we do not receive the truth of righteousness, it has the effect of dominoes falling—we continue to live in a poverty mindset as though it is godly. As a consequence of that, we never enter the status of sonship, or heirs, because we are still living as slaves. This in turn means that the church has a mindset of waiting for tomorrow as though God will do something more *then*.

Today is not a day of grace and salvation despite the fact that Jesus has declared it so! Instead, we remain in a mindset that thinks…*one day* we will be healed, and *one day* Jesus will finish things off.… When we get to Heaven, everything will be fine, but right now we just have to grin and bear it. Believers sing songs and pray prayers that say all the right things—or nearly—but exercise no faith; therefore, even though He hears, He is unable to actually answer in the way He so desires.

The Church is waiting for God to act and blames Him for its own wrong choices. Immaturity keeps it from taking responsibility for anything that it has or does do, choosing rather to find other scapegoats. Even though the truth is that we have everything we could possibly need, we act as though we have nothing and seldom even thank Him for all that He has already done.

You may ask, is this really the way the Church is? Sadly, I think that this mindset includes about 90 percent of the Church today. I find that the majority of those who are the Church don't really know what they believe, and quite honestly, they don't seem to really care. This is why we need a reformation not just a refreshing or revival.

Jesus has a blueprint for life that we might have fullness of life, but if we don't understand the directives and disciplines that help us find that life and live in it, then we will only live half a life with half the love and power that is available—and we probably won't enjoy much of it either!

On Earth as in Heaven

Just as Paul had a great battle to contend for the true faith, we too have this same fight. Christianity is about *life*—living life for Jesus. It is not about meetings, programs, rules, and regulations. It's about living life to the max, in relationship with the Author of life and the King of the universe—a King who is full of life and love, who has no lack of grace and is always growing and filling everything with more of His life.

There are thousands and millions of Christians today who are as saved as you and I. When they leave this earth, they will be brought into the glory of His wonderful presence. It will be a wonderful place. But Jesus Himself desired, wanted, expected, and showed us that His Kingdom could come here upon the earth. He never intended for us to wait until then. He tore the curtain that separated us from His presence "behold, the veil of the temple curtain was torn in two from top to bottom; and the earth quaked..." (Matt. 27:51), and He came to get us. His Holy Spirit so desired us that He came after us, found us, loved us, and filled us with His life. He is being poured out today, not tomorrow, not next year, but **today** and every day thereafter called today.

It is finished. What more can He do? It's all been accomplished, it's all done. Sin is taken away. He cannot and will not do anything more. It's all written in His last will and testament—the greatest, most wonderful legal document ever written or witnessed anywhere, either in Heaven or upon the earth.

FULLNESS OF LIFE

The great fruit of apostolic doctrine is that it does away with sin consciousness and brings you into your standing as the righteousness of God in Christ Jesus. This doctrine of righteousness is meant to be a fundamental teaching within the Church, "For everyone who partakes only of milk is unskilled in the word of righteousness, for he is a babe" (Heb. 5:13). Yet most of the Church does not receive it. This is a grievous matter. Apostolic teaching is meant to release us from living a life of rules and regulations—of living the law and replaces it with the law of the Spirit of life in Christ Jesus, "For the law of the Spirit of life in Christ Jesus has made me free from the law of sin and death" (Rom. 8:2), which is all about fullness of life and learning to overcome. This is what the blueprint of life is all about.

It also releases to you faith, which is found in the Author and One who perfects our faith, and helps you exercise it to grow and increase the measure you have been given. This is real faith that takes you beyond fear. As you come to know the love of God, and fear is extracted from your life, you begin to see yourself a son or daughter who lives to serve, not as a slave, because you have been given the full inheritance of the firstborn. Apostolic teaching continually reminds you of building in a right way the way of wisdom. When you see Him more clearly, your ego does not inflict itself upon you and others, shouting its own praise. In place of misery and poverty, you become praise to His glorious grace, living to give and not to get.

True Christianity

The truth is that most Christians still live in an Old Testament dispensation. The Christianity they practice is not apostolic doctrine that is New Testament Christianity. It's an "in-betweeny old and meany" kind of Christianity—religious falsehood parading itself, giving an appearance of wisdom, but lacking real power and abundant life. Its repentance is not real, and therefore, those who practice it cannot live the life of Christ, no matter how much they say they will or pray that they might.

You might well be thinking that I am painting a very sad and desperate picture. Please let me reassure you that while a great percentage of the Church does actually look like this, there is a deep and real hunger within many hearts that have been and continue to seek out what is real and true. Nothing will stop what Christ paid so dearly for. Nothing can or will overcome the Church.

As we begin to align ourselves with all that God says about us and all that He has done for us in ever increasing measure, as we seek to implement by His Spirit the directives and disciplines that He has given so that we might live in His blueprint for our lives, then we will experience true reformation and the fullness of the life He has for us that comes forth in the power of God!

Chapter Six

FATHERING SONS

It is important to understand that the subject of master craftsmen and women is all about building—not the building of wood or stone houses—but rather the *internal* building of individual lives and of those lives being built together as a spiritual house, which brings glory to the Lord Jesus. Because this work of building individual lives is integral to the work of an apostle, in this chapter I examine the nature of apostolic fathering.

I realize that all fathers are not necessarily apostles; however, I do believe that *all apostles should be fathers*, and that the natural course of growing up builds every true son into a genuine father. There are fathers who may not be given to the body as apostles, but those who are called apostles, must have learned, or be learning, to be fathers to those whom they are helping to build. To more fully appreciate what a father may look like, we must understand how a person who is called to be a disciple of Jesus can experience the fullness of being a father in the faith.

Building and *transformation* are the plans within the blueprint for all who are called to follow Jesus. Nothing has changed since He walked on the earth, other than the way we may think about how God wants to do things. *His process remains the same.*

The truth is, you are expected to change, but not in your own strength, or by your own means—that is why He has so thoroughly changed us within. We know that we cannot do it without Him! He has given us not only a new heart, but also a new spirit, His Holy Spirit and His Word "I will give you a new heart and put a new spirit within you; I will take the heart of stone out of your flesh and give you a heart of flesh. I will put My Spirit within you and cause you to walk in My statutes, and you will keep My judgments and do them" (Ezek. 36:26-27). Because of this, He is able to direct our thoughts and teach us throughout each day. This is the total, fantastic package we receive when we accept His gift of salvation, and it includes everything we need to make the changes required of us.

In the end, we will be transformed by His Spirit; we will be built into all that He has created and designed us to become. That's His bottom line. He doesn't create second-rate, or secondhand stuff. *You are His best and He wants His best for you.*

THE WAY TO SONSHIP

As discussed previously, when Jesus called men and women to Himself, He first called them to be *disciples*. (I write about discipleship in great depth in my book, *Constructional Truth*.) The way to sonship is through discipleship; apostolic teaching is about making disciples, and Jesus' last words instructed His followers to go into all the world making disciples.

We can define a disciple as: *someone who is bound to another, in love; to learn a craft; or, one who learns in submission to teaching and under discipline.* In this day and age, the idea of discipleship is not readily embraced by many, and is often "picked to bits," in an attempt to undermine the idea. Nonetheless, for those of us who serve Jesus and are citizens of His Kingdom, *discipleship is not optional*—like it or not, He will disciple those who are His. This is all part of the blueprint for life. As the writer to the Hebrews makes clear, if you are without discipline you are illegitimate, "But if you are without chastening, of which all have become partakers, then you are illegitimate and not sons" (Heb. 12:8).

Imagine if you were to leave this earth today and enter into the Kingdom of Heaven, there will be great rejoicing there upon your arrival. You will be welcomed with love and overwhelming joy! However, I do not think that you will be let loose to do whatever you might want or choose to do. Initially, you will need time just to adjust to new surroundings and the incredible light and love of that place. There might even be some places and people that you will not be able to see or meet right away simply because your eyes and ears are not be accustomed to the Kingdom. Also, you will need to be properly clothed, strengthened, and taught the proper way to enter into God's presence.

Choosing to cooperate with the Holy Spirit on earth helps prepare us not only to live a full life here but also as those who will be citizens of Heaven, in the Kingdom of God.

Discipleship Now Prepares Us for Then

We are free to choose to be stubborn and rebellious *now*, rather than to learn and develop as disciples; but, whether you like it or not, either *now* or *then* (and you should like it) you will be transformed to fit as citizens of a heavenly Kingdom so that you can meet the King! Theoretically we are free not to cooperate with the Holy Spirit in changing our lives; however, choosing disobedience and lawlessness may disqualify us in the end.

That is the reason Jesus called His followers to discipleship, and that is why we have been called to the exact same thing—to get us ready for what is to come. It's a different Kingdom, with a humble King of mercy, grace, and love—the lawless and rebellious will not stand in His presence. Discipleship not only prepares you to walk worthy in the here and now, but also readies you for your entry into glory.

You are called into the same calling as the followers of Christ who walked the earth with Him! As you learn to hear His voice, see who He really is, and follow Him through the enabling and life of the Holy Spirit, you will begin to fall in love with Him. In this process of learning who He is and loving Him, He will begin to ask you to do some things that may be uncomfortable or difficult for you. He will ask you to serve, and do things not just for Him, but also for others.

He may ask you to help with what seems to be silly little things—things that no one sees or ever hears about. You may sometimes feel as though these things are below you somehow. But these *silly, little things* will find you out; in other words, they will reveal to you what is in your own heart. You may find yourself reacting or responding in bad ways, even surprising yourself by some of the things that you do or say.

What began as a wonderful, exciting experience in your walk with the Lord begins to wear off, and you may find yourself feeling tired and weary. You may even struggle with feeling used, but through it all you will be learning many things about yourself, about God's great love and grace, and His desire and ability to change you by His Word and through His Spirit. You will begin to see both yourself and Him more clearly—you will also begin to see others in the light of His love and grace—and you will begin to understand His Kingdom more and more as you learn to serve, here, there, and everywhere. As you experience His love in all these various situations, you begin to realize that, slowly but surely, you are growing up, maturing.

Obedience, submission, and *love,* that's what discipleship is all about; all part of the blueprint of life. We are called to be like Him. We are not just called to *do what He does,* but we are called to *be like He is,* and that is the true meaning of this important word *discipleship.* People often think that it is too harsh or hard of a word for these days, but I believe it is an important word that we cannot lose. Many would rather we call this process encouragement, or mentoring, or even being apprenticed, but none of these words suffice to explain what God means to do through this process. Only *discipleship* fits because it includes things that we experience and learn from, things meant to become a permanent part of who we are.

SERVANTHOOD AND OBEDIENCE

Servanthood is an attitude of the heart that overtakes the mind. We never stop serving. No matter what we become, where we go, or what we do; for those who love Christ, serving will always be an important part of our lives. After all, the purpose of discipleship is to make us like Jesus—the only Son of God, the Creator of the earth whose whole being is one of sacrificial servanthood. All of Heaven is filled with this same heart and nature, we can't get in the door apart from a humble heart like Jesus', full of love and eager to serve; and we certainly could not be comfortable there any other way.

As we serve, certain things begin to happen. Our obedience to His command and Word are tested. Will we do as the Master's commands, or will we do our own thing, being led by our own understanding rather than His Spirit and Truth?

SERVING SONS

We know that we are made sons and daughters of God through faith in Christ upon receiving His gift of salvation.

For you are all sons of God through faith in Christ Jesus (Galatians 3:26).

However, He desires that we know sonship not only as a faith fact, but also as an actual experience, a present-day reality that involves a deep sense of knowing in the center of our being that we are real, true sons of the living God. The only way we can really know this sort of sonship is through obedience, which requires faith working through love. You can *say* that you love Him as a son, but the only way you really *know* that you love Him is that you obey His Word. In the same way, He knows that what you say about loving Him is true.

If you love Me keep my commandments (John 14:15).

He who does not love Me does not keep my commandments (John 14:24).

Again, we need to remind ourselves that when we received our new hearts and He recreated our spirits within us, at that very same time He put His Spirit within us and filled our hearts with His love. He did all of this so that we could walk in His statutes and fulfill His commands. Thus we can love Him and keep His commands because of the work of His Spirit within us.

The only way that you know you love Him is when you are obedient to His commands—*that is the only way*. Our words, after all, are just words. But the truth of those words is tested and proven by our actions, when He asks us to do something according to how He thinks about it and wants it done—not according to our desires and thoughts about it.

> **Discipleship teaches us how to serve and brings us from a position of service into friendship.**

So, discipleship teaches us how to serve, what obedience and submission are, and brings us from a position of service into friendship. We don't stop serving, we come to understand that servanthood is something that flows together with and out of love toward the godhead and to others around us. It becomes a *normal* part of our nature and way of thinking just as it is the Father's.

SERVANTS AND FRIENDS

As Jesus discipled His followers, the result was that through their submission and obedience to His Word they became His friends and this is what He said about them:

> *You are My friends if you do whatever I command you. No longer do I call you servants, for a servant does not know what his master is doing; but I have called you friends, for all things that I heard from My father I have made known to you* (John 15:14-15).

As they walked faithfully with Jesus, He began to see that He could trust them. They were no longer merely servants; by their service they had shown Him that He could not only *ask things of them,* but that He could *also reveal things to them* and trust them to carry out instructions with His same Spirit of love and grace. Beyond that, He knew that He could trust them to live displaying His nature in all they did, because they were always cooperating in the process of becoming more like Him.

Jesus desires all who follow Him to be trustworthy with the secrets of His Kingdom. He wants to show and tell us all that He has done and all that He will do to bring about His fullness upon the earth. A servant does not know the depths of His master's heart, but a bond servant—one who has shown that he can be trusted and responsible in all things pertaining to the King's household—is someone who can be given greater access into the realms of not only the Father's house, *but more importantly, the Father's heart.* The result of this process is that we too can become sons to the Father in experiential reality and also eventually as fathers to those around us.

SERVANTS, FRIENDS, AND SONS

During Jesus' time on earth, He became a pattern for us. He not only gave to us a blueprint for life, He exemplified that blueprint, setting a good example and teaching His followers how to be faithful and behave as true children of God. He also showed them how to become a father who could build individual lives and help knit them together for the sake of His Kingdom.

> *Jesus said to him, "Have I been with you so long, and yet you have not known Me Philip? He who has seen Me has seen the Father; so how can you say, 'Show us the Father'? Do you not believe that I am in the Father, and the Father in Me? The words that I speak to you I do not speak on My own authority; but the Father who dwells in Me does the works* (John 14:9-10).

Clearly Jesus was not *just* a Rabbi to them. He was not just a Master teaching His craft. Rather, He was a *Father* to them as they walked with Him. He was building them internally, designing their inner spirit into a house fit for a King. With great wisdom He furnished their homes as a dwelling place for His life and purpose. This was the great Apostle using all His tools as a Master Craftsman within the context of relationship.

Relationship — the Heart of God

It is clear that God the Father does not do anything without absolute unity with God the Son and God the Spirit. The three are in relationship as One—Their hearts beat with the same love, and They think with the same attitude of mind. The three are in relationship with one another—living and breathing together. *Everything God does is about relationship.* He doesn't form organizations, clubs, networks, or associations. He builds heart relationships. Throughout the Word He is revealed as a God of relationship who puts us in families, brings forth children, and raises up households.

In this day and age when the Church is doing everything it can to become relevant to a dying world, it must also be watchful not to compromise the foundational truths that are established in the very heart of God. *There can be no substitute for relationship.* Although there was, no doubt, networking done through deep heart relationships, that was not God's primary purpose; for apart from true relationship there could be no effectual networking at all! We must remember that God can and will use everything He can use, He will bless everything He can bless, that does not mean that it is His best or that He is approving of it. It just displays His amazing goodness and grace, for which we are tremendously grateful.

> **There can be no substitute for relationship.**

Jesus fathered His followers through discipleship, which included *servanthood into friendship* and *friendship into sonship*. But He didn't stop there; He proceeded to bring them into a double blessing.

Initially, Jesus furnished their inner spirits, "Wisdom has built her house…" (Prov. 9:1). He then transformed and restored their thinking through His Word and by His Spirit. He dealt with their hearts' intentions and motivations, and disciplined them in the things of the Kingdom. He reprogrammed them, so to speak, but before He could fully empower them, the old hard drive had to be removed. They could never attain the purpose of God with the old one (heart) in place. Even though they were hearing, seeing, and experiencing the Kingdom with Jesus, they couldn't fully grasp it—not until He died on the cross.

That was the final lesson, the greatest and most difficult one of all. *At Calvary He showed them by example that His purposes in the Kingdom are accomplished from the place of death.* In other words, we must give up self-interest and lay down our lives to allow the fullness of His life to live in and through us. As the disciples witnessed this firsthand, their own dreams, desires, thoughts, and ideas of destiny—even those they thought were for the sake of His Kingdom—came tumbling down.

Only then could receive a new soft drive—a new heart.

> *So Jesus said to them again, "Peace to you! As the Father has sent Me, I also send you." And when He had said this, He breathed on them, and said to them, "Receive the Holy Spirit"* (John 20:21-22).

Then they were born again. They could not be born again apart from the finished work of Christ on the cross and in the resurrection. Only afterward could they be saved and only after they were born again could they fully understand and see how all the new programs that He had installed on the inside of them would actually operate in the fullness of His purpose. Now they could really live His blueprint for their lives.

So the first step of apostolic fathering is to build internally those whom the Lord gives, individually and corporately. And this all takes place through *relationship*. Yes, it's about *master and servant,* but it's also about *father and child.* I am absolutely certain this is the Kingdom way of doing things, and this is how Jesus wants it done. There is a pattern, and when we find it, it is best to build using it.

Chapter Seven

Spiritual Sons'
Perspectives and Honor

The following testimonies are written by two young men whom I have had the pleasure to father over the years.

A Fatherless Son

My journey began at the age of 15. It was a warm, sunny afternoon and I was playing my favorite sport. Baseball of course! My heart was heavy that day as 18 months earlier I got the news that Dad had colon cancer. We walked in faith and believed for healing as a family, but when I saw Grandpa's car pulling up to the baseball field, I knew something was wrong. Dad had been on death's doorstep for the past few days, and without a miracle there was no hope. When I saw my grandpa, I knew that the moment of saying good-bye to my dad for the last time was drawing near.

I remember the feeling of hopelessness that came over me in that moment as the thought of losing my dad really started to hit home. I arrived home and saw my dad in a comatose state. I simply held his hand and prayed.

Watching someone die is an interesting experience. Watching Dad pass on to Heaven was something I can't really describe. I didn't feel extreme pain or despair in that moment, I just felt deadened. It was in this moment that my journey began. It wasn't a journey that I was consciously aware of, but simply a heart that had a need, a need for a father to teach him the ways of life and walk with him through it. Now, I wouldn't have verbalized that at that time in that way, but it was the un-avoidable truth that every son needs a father.

We all know that God is a Father to the fatherless, and He is for me, but the Bible also says that there are many teachers but very few fathers. This isn't a void that you are aware of until it happens. The truth is that no matter if you have a father or not, we all need to have the heart of a son.

In one sense, I wasn't fatherless. God was looking after me all of the time. This is much easier to say now with ten years of hindsight than it would have been at that time. As I look back on the experience of being without a father, I can see the moments when God met my needs, whether through someone or simply teaching me via life experience. There were many moments when my heart was crying out for a father, but in the midst of the pain, God was moving and bringing good from all of it. He always does.

God Brings an Earthly Father

About six years later, Paul Hubbard came into my life. My family had been going through some difficult times since the death of Dad, and Paul felt it was right to fly all of us from our home in the States to England to be with the church for a two-week vacation. I'm not sure he understood at that time how much of a lifesaver that was for all of us, particularly my mom. It was a wonderful time with Christian Life Church in England, and I went back for another visit in October. It was during that visit that Paul began to talk to me about living in England, working with the church, and being raised up as a spiritual son.

Over the years growing up, I knew that I was called to be involved in church ministry. Besides the countless words spoken over my life, it was something in my heart. When Paul mentioned this opportunity, it resonated with what God placed on my heart and I quickly said yes. It wasn't until June of the next year that I made it over to "sunny England."

Thankfully I didn't know all that being a son meant or all that I would go through during my time in England, or I probably wouldn't have accepted. It is, of course, all worth it and God knows exactly what He is doing, but it isn't always easy! Even when God places us with a spiritual father on this earth, in the end it is God who is doing the majority of the fathering. He has taught me so many lessons and brought me through so much in my almost four years here. It isn't over yet, but I am starting to reap the rewards of this walk of sonship.

My Journey

I remember being so excited about going to England. I had plenty of confirmation; and when the day finally came, I was more than ready to go. Upon my arrival, I didn't really know what to expect. I knew that I was going to be a son to Paul, trained by him and the church. But what I knew in my head and my emotional experience were two very different things. I remember being somewhat nervous around Paul. I wouldn't have been able to identify it at that time, but there was always a tension there for me. As time went on and I spent more and more time with Paul, I began to notice that when I was with him I was fine, but when I knew I was meeting with him or knew something was coming up, there was a tension I carried. I started to realize that in my head I knew that Paul loved me and cared for me, but it didn't connect with my heart. The mental assent was there, but I didn't have the knowing via experience. When you lose a father as some of us know, it can be challenging to feel secure around male authority figures. But in the relationship of a father to a son it goes a step further.

When God thinks of fathers and sons, He always thinks of the heart. In Malachi 4 it says, "He will turn the hearts of the fathers to their children, and the hearts of the children to their fathers." This reflects how God thinks when He thinks in terms of fathers and sons. God required that I not only understand that I was a son to Paul, but also that my heart was given to him. This task isn't very easy for most people, especially someone who has lost a father or who has a difficult relationship with their dad. You learn to protect your heart by keeping part of it locked away; but when God asks you to be a son to Him, He wants all of your heart, not just your mental assent, and He puts those same expectations on our earthly relationships.

As the first year went by, I realized that I had this discomfort around Paul. I asked myself all kinds of questions: *Is this Paul's fault? Is it something he is doing? Is it something I am doing? What should I do differently?* But no matter how long I thought about it, I couldn't figure it out. All of my mental strength wasn't enough to conquer this problem. As the second year in England started to go by with slight reprieve and a bit less tension, I got to a point where I gave up trying to figure it out and just said, "OK God, You have to help me with this one." What I didn't realize is that the whole time He was helping me. He was bringing me to a place where I could deal with this issue and change from the inside out.

No matter all of the fears and struggles I had on the inside, Paul stuck with me. It didn't matter what I did, or what I didn't do, he was there for me and never gave up. Over time, this began to sink in. I slowly started to believe that this guy really does love me. I didn't realize that all along it was nothing to do with him but everything to do with me not understanding how to give my heart to a father. This also meant I didn't understand how to fully give my heart to my heavenly Dad.

It took about two and a half years but all of the sudden I noticed a shift on the inside of me. I noticed that I was no longer nervous around Paul and when I thought of him my heart began to smile. I couldn't help but be happy. Instead of tension when I knew I had a meeting with him, I felt joy! It didn't stop there, though. Paul's example showed me that no matter what, God loved me in the midst of everything. It was something that I had mental assent to for most of my life, but had never experienced. Through Paul's love for me it became clear that God feels the same about me—except much more so.

At this point, I realized that my heart was being carried by a father. This was a whole new world! To be a true son, I had to know that I was carried on the heart of my father. This set me free to be me in a way I never thought possible. I saw clearly that God is my Father and just how Paul carries me on his heart, God does the same, regardless of what I feel or do.

Knowing this began to affect everything I did. The youth, leading, preaching, serving, and everything I was involved in began to change. Instead of just doing a good job, I began to carry people on my heart the same way I realized I was being carried. Everything I did went up a level. Instead of just leading the youth, or preaching on a Sunday, my heart was "carrying" people and my ability to love people increased greatly. This part of the journey was key for me and brought me into levels of love and freedom I didn't know existed. It was obvious to me that I was lacking something, and I had a great desire for it, but what I didn't realize is that all along God was bringing me into a deeper understanding of His love for me. More than just an experience or a momentary glimpse, but teaching me something that is now part of who I am and therefore cannot be taken from me.

Borrowing Identity

There were many times I didn't understand how loved I was as a son and how I was truly cared for. I went into a meeting with Paul feeling tense and came out feeling fantastic, like I was on top on the world. After a while I realized that I was borrowing his love and peace. These things were part of who he is, not things that he acted like he had but actually part of the makeup of his character. They weren't part of my character yet so I would effectively "borrow" them from him. After a while these "on top of the world" feelings would fade and I would wonder, *Where did they go?* It was a great frustration, but after this revelation that I am carried on his heart as well as the heart of my heavenly Dad, this love became mine. I no longer needed to borrow it from Paul; I could now lend it to others. So instead of giving something to others that I borrowed, I am able to give love and peace to others that is my own.

It began to go a step further as this new secure love that I was experiencing started to shape my identity. The simple act of truly giving my heart to Father God began to revolutionize my life. I could see clearly that my identity was being formed and shaped by this revelation and it suddenly became a lot easier to simply be me.

This journey isn't always easy. There have been many times that have required submission, patience, grace, and tested me to the limit. But when I look back, I realize that God has placed me with a great father and is shaping me into a true son. This hasn't been an easy journey in many ways, and there were many times when I felt like quitting, times when it would have been far easier to simply give up.

When I didn't realize that I was "carried" on Paul's heart, it was easy to misunderstand what he said and read into his actions in a way that didn't accurately reflect his thoughts toward me. It was easy to misjudge him and others, and I could have easily been a stumbling block to myself. The pain of the journey could have deterred me from getting to the reward, but in the end God knew and has kept me in the midst of it all. I have had to deal with some difficult things, make some decisions that everything in my soul was telling me not to make, and stick it out no matter what, but it has all been worth it.

Now I have a true father because I am a true son. He was always a true father; I just wasn't a true son. I now feel love and care for my earthly dad and my heavenly Father in a way that I never thought possible. In the end, I have had to deal with myself, face fears, anxieties, anger, and frustrations, but God has brought me great reward by showing me what it means to be a true son.

—Isaac Rowe

FATHERING ME

In 2004, Paul saw the potential in me to become the man of God I am now and will become in the future. His heart was to release me into that future through fathering me in the Lord. The potential he saw in me has been and continues to be realized in my life for the benefit of the Kingdom of God.

Since the time we agreed to walk together, I have walked with Paul as a son to a father in the Lord. Paul has walked with me every step of the way over these past five years. Through the ups and the downs and all the challenges of life, he has been with me and alongside me. It has been a very challenging walk and there were a few times when I was tempted to walk away. He initially invited me to walk with him in this way, but every day I must choose to continue the relationship. I have never been coerced or manipulated in any way, shape, or form. If I want to, I have every right to walk away.

Paul has never once told me what to do—which has annoyed me greatly on a number of occasions!—because he understands that true fathering is never about control, but always about release. He will guide and suggest, but every decision I have made has been mine and mine alone.

What is it like to be fathered in this way? It means knowing that you are loved for who you are yet challenged to be who you can become. It means being accountable in every area of life and being open and honest about what really goes on when no one but the Lord is looking. It means having someone who has gone through the trial and tribulations of ministry to bounce ideas off and to share the pain.

Walking together has brought great joys as well as pain. I remember one year receiving a letter from him with his thoughts on the past year. It was five typed pages with one page of encouragement and four pages of things I needed to deal with, both in the church and in my personal life. I did not like him that day! And yet I loved him for it. I had asked to be accountable and said that I wanted to learn—so he taught me. And I recall His words when he handed me the letter, "You're doing great, this is because I want the best for you. Don't get down about the contents; be encouraged, we are only dealing with the ten percent that is not quite right."

I can say from personal experience that the words written in this book are not just theory. I have walked in them and can personally testify that this is how Paul lives. The thoughts and beliefs that he has written come not from his head, but from his heart. He lives and breathes these things, and I have been extremely privileged to have benefited from them.

This is the fathering I have experienced. I have been loved, released, cared for, looked after, and pushed out into the deep, challenged and never manipulated or coerced into anything. In short, I have been loved by a man with a pure heart, who loves Jesus and the Kingdom of God above all else.

It is a great honor and privilege to call him my spiritual dad.

—Adam Carver

The Truth About Honor

I believe that the foundational practice of honor is lacking in the church today; and the truth is, if we do not honor our fathers and leaders, then we are not honoring God, "Do you not know that those who minister the holy things eat of the things of the temple, and those who serve at the altar partake of the offerings of the altar? Even so the Lord has commanded that those who preach the gospel should live from the gospel. But I have used none of these things, nor have I written these things that it should be done so to me; for it would be better for me to die than that anyone should make my boasting void" (1 Cor. 9:13-15).

Paul's boast was that he lived his life totally given over to the Lord. He chose to use all he had and everything he was to fulfill his commission. In the end, he could boast that despite all the odds, *despite* being dishonored and disrespected, *despite* being persecuted, run out of town, misunderstood and misaligned, in the end he would stand before the Lord and testify that none of that had stopped him from fulfilling the great commission that he had received—that was *his* choice.

Many churches and leaders have made this choice for their pastors, for those who serve them. They have decided that it is spiritual for the man or woman of God, the one who has been called and chosen to do whatever is necessary to follow Jesus. *They* (the people) have decided that in order to keep their minister holy, to check his or her motives and calling out, *they* have decided that *they* will not honor that person—in many places not even pay them a decent living wage. This is all done in the name of Christ. People truly believe that they are exercising spiritual wisdom to keep their ministers humble!

However these actions and attitudes are not from wisdom and have nothing to do with Christ or His Kingdom. Neither do they have anything to do with humility or spirituality. They are abominations before the Lord, and those who make such decisions and rules will be dealt with most severely in the end; because the truth is that, "Even so the Lord has commanded that those who preach the gospel should live from the gospel" (1 Cor. 9:14).

True sons and daughters of God will always seek to honor those who minister the life of Christ to them. Those who realize that they have had fathers and teachers who unfolded to them the blueprint of life, who helped them see who they really are and become the person God intended them to become, those will always seek to honor them who ministered this life to them.

Apostolic ministry births sons and daughters who honor.

I have written about the relationship that apostolic life reproduces within the church elsewhere in this book. Just as we read earlier, true sons bring honor to their Father. The apostle Paul speaks of his apostolic life demonstrating both motherly and fatherly characteristics toward those in its care.

> *Nor did we seek glory from men, either from you or from others, when we might have made demands as apostles of Christ. But we were gentle among you, just as a nursing mother cherishes her own children. So affectionately longing for you, we were well pleased to impart to you not only the gospel of God, but also our own lives, because you had become dear to us. For you remember brethren, our labor and toil; for laboring night and day, that we might not be a burden to any of you, we preached the gospel of God. You are witnesses, and God also, how devoutly and justly and blamelessly we behaved ourselves among you who believe; as you know how we exhorted and comforted and charged every one of you, as a father does his children, that you would walk worthy of God, who calls you into His own kingdom and glory* (1 Thessalonians 2:6-12).

Apostolic life primarily calls into discipleship those who truly want to follow Jesus. Included in discipling is servanthood, which also draws us into sonship. As a result, the knowledge of being sons through faith in Christ Jesus becomes an actual reality in our daily lives. We learn how to live as sons, and sons eventually become fathers. However, it is impossible to be a good father without first having been a good son. It is equally impossible to become a good master without having been a good servant.

> **When the Church walks in the maturity of its inheritance, it will automatically bring forth honor.**

When the Church grows up and begins to walk in maturity as sons of our inheritance, then it will automatically bring forth honor. However, we must understand that it is impossible to give honor to the Father in Heaven if we are not giving honor to our fathers on earth. Everything that we experience as a spiritual reality must also be a reality to us on earth. If we say we love the Father and Jesus, then we must love one another, or the truth is not in us. If we say that we trust the Father but do not trust one another, then we are liars. In like manner, if we say we honor our father in Heaven, but show no honor to fathers on earth, the truth is not in us.

TO HONOR IS NATURAL

It is worth noting that true sons learn to honor just as they learn to serve. Eventually it becomes a normal and integral part of them. They do not serve or honor because the Father demands it from them; rather, it becomes something they do naturally.

Fathers who have to coerce their sons into doing what they should automatically do will sooner or later have a problem. Speaking of this, the apostle Paul said:

> *For what is it in which you were inferior to other churches, except that I myself was not burdensome to you? Forgive me this wrong! Now for the third time I am ready to come to you. And I will not be burdensome to you; for I do not seek yours, but you. For the children ought not to lay up for the parents, but the parents for the children. And I will very gladly spend and be spent for your souls; though the more abundantly I love you, the less I am loved. But be that as it may, I did not burden you...* (2 Corinthians 12:13-16).

Clearly, Paul is saying that, as a father, his heart is toward his children. He will give and give and give; in fact, he says that the more he loves them the less he is loved by them! Again, this is so sad, so desperately grievous to the Holy Spirit, to see His chosen servants who are so sacrificial and giving be completely taken for granted.

There is no sense at all in the Scriptures that Paul was coercing his children, his sons, or the churches to meet his needs. Even though that should be the heart response of the people, and the correct way in which a minister and father of the gospel should be honored, yet he did not demand it of them. He simply instructed them, letting them know about it—but in the end it was their choice. I have no doubt he was praying and hoping that they would want to meet all his material and financial needs, not only for his own sake, but for theirs.

Chapter Eight

SONS TO FATHERS

THE DOUBLE PORTION

The Father is not merely interested in raising up sons who will have an inheritance, though that is good; neither is He interested in raising children living on single portions of His blessing. He is, however, very interested in giving them *double* portions, *abundant* blessings, an *overflow* of all that He has for them!

We look at the talents and abilities that are displayed in the church and consider ourselves as charismatic and gifted; in general, we believe that we are in the Spirit. However, I believe that being filled with the Spirit is much more than merely displaying our God-given gifts and abilities! It is much more than speaking in tongues, prophesying, and seeing people healed. These are all wonderful, but by no means is this the fullness of what God intends for us. That is merely paddling in the river as opposed to being submerged in the depths of our God! This may be acceptable for the vast majority of believers. However, it will never suffice for those who are hungry and thirsty for God and want to truly enter into the fullness of sonship here on earth. The fullness of God is displayed in its greatness not by what we do, but by our nature and character, by *who* we become as sons and daughters of the living God.

> *But if you bite and devour one another, beware lest you be consumed by one another! I say then; Walk in the Spirit and you shall not fulfill the lust of the flesh...if you are led by the Spirit you are not under the law.... But the fruit of the Spirit is love,*

joy, peace, longsuffering, kindness, goodness, faithfulness, gentleness, self-control. Against such there is not law (Galatians 5:15-16,18,22).

In review, the first thing the Master Craftsman does is build us internally thereby enabling the Holy Spirit to dwell in every room of our spiritual house—filling us with the Spirit within.

Do you not know that your body is the temple of the Holy Spirit who is in you, whom you have from God, and you are not your own (1 Corinthians 6:19).

Second, He empowers us with an overwhelming flow of His Spirit, which refills us internally and anoints us externally with power.

But you shall receive power when the Holy Spirit has come upon you; and you shall be witnesses to Me in Jerusalem, in all Judea and Samaria, and to the end of the earth (Acts 1:8).

In the same way that Elisha received the double blessing of inheritance (see 2 Kings 2:9), so do those who are true sons of the Kingdom. This kind of power is the rightful inheritance of every son of the Kingdom. When we walk in this kind of life and power, we are truly beginning to walk in the blueprint of life. This is the pattern that Jesus set before us; this life and power is what He enjoyed upon the earth.

Far too few enjoy this kind of life. I believe this failure is due to the fact that the "house within" is not built sufficiently so that it can contain and run with that degree of dynamic, explosive power. And in order for this sort of building to take place, we need apostolic fathers who will lay down their lives to invest in building others.

FATHERS IN TRUTH

Before any man can be a father to a son (in the true spiritual sense) he himself must be a son. Before any man can be a master he must first be a servant. A good example from the Bible is Elisha who had been a servant first; as he served he became a son to his spiritual father, Elijah, who was also his master. In the end, he received a double portion as he cried out, "My Father, My Father..." Shortly afterward Elisha became both a master and a father to those who would follow and learn from him. Like Elisha, our hearts need to be turned toward our fathers and vice versa, then we will be ready to walk into our future. (See First Kings 2.)

Although there are numerous natural fathers in the church—those who have fathered children naturally—there are not so many spiritual fathers, "For though you might have ten thousand instructors in Christ, yet you do not have many fathers; for in Christ Jesus I have begotten you through the gospel. Therefore I urge you, imitate me" (1 Cor. 4:15-16). Many natural fathers in the Church who are older and have experienced life like to think that this qualifies them as fathers to younger men and women in the Body of Christ. They see themselves as wise sages who can bring counsel.

However, many of them do not understand or perceive rightly about what it means to father others in the Lord. Although they may be fathers in the natural and have experienced many things pertaining to life, they often lack heavenly wisdom and their minds have not been transformed by the Word of God. This is clear because many of them do not have relationship within the Body. They have never experienced sonship themselves, or learned how to walk in that relationship and therefore could never (remaining in that position) be fathers in the church.

Wisdom does not come from the passing of years, although you can become wise as the years pass. Wisdom comes as we have our minds transformed by the Word of God and become an obedient and submitted son, both to the Father in Heaven, and also to those who father us on earth.

Longevity

As mentioned previously, the Lord has always worked in and through relationship. The Bible is based around a relationship involving a Son and His Father, and it is filled with family matters. Abraham, the father of our faith, received a vision from God; the only way that he would fulfill His call to become a multitude was through a son. *If we don't want the vision to die within a generation, we must raise up sons, otherwise it will die with us.*

In the past there has been much talk about how God loves everything BIG. In the beginning, He created everything and caused it to multiply, placing the ability to reproduce within each seed. Of course, the Lord does things on a huge scale, but we must understand that bigness or great numbers in themselves are *not* what please God.

> **What pleases God is reproduction by faith through love in relationship.**

Although it is true that there may be huge churches where every seat is taken, in the end it is what is planted into individual hearts and what that seed of God's life then reproduces into other lives that is crucial. If it is truly God, then not only will it live, but it will reproduce in the next generation, and in fact, be handed down to many coming generations. If every congregation of 100 raised up father/son relationships, it would reproduce both disciples and sons for the coming generations. The end result would be far in excess of anything that a mega church may have enjoyed for years. All its ministers, associated ministries, and works would also raise up disciples and sons who in turn would be fathers, and all this would cause massive reproduction and fruitfulness. The best, of course, would be to have mega churches that reproduced in the way just outlined.

As I have often said to my own children, "My ceiling should be your floor." What I have fought hard for, what I have pioneered, and what has cost me much, the vision that I carry is the inheritance I am passing on to them upon which they can build and add.

Jesus is our example. He was and is the Son of God, but He was also the son of a man, Joseph. It is evident that He was totally submitted to His Father in Heaven, but likewise He was also submitted to His earthly parents, "Then He went down with them and came to Nazareth, and was subject to them..." (Luke 2:51).

Sowing Into God's Order

The kingdom of heaven is like a grain of mustard seed, which a man took and sowed into his field: which indeed is the least of all the seeds, but when it is grown, it is the greatest among herbs and becometh a tree... (Matthew 13:31-32 KJV).

When a man sows, he reaps; and what a man sows, so shall he reap. Although it may take significant time before the seed turns into a tree, when a man sows into the order of sonship by raising sons, then the seed continues to reproduce and each generation becomes stronger and greater. Only as we raise sons of the same order can our ministry produce great fruit and continue. *And only when we have a generation of true sons can true fathers take their place.*

For example, if a man took ten disciples, and gave himself to the task of raising them up as sons, and then they all did it with another ten men, over the course of twelve years he could have as many as 12,000 disciples! Given thirty years, he could reach an entire city or touch a whole nation!

This principle is often scorned and rejected within the church, because we do not like to wait patiently for anything anymore, and it seems as though we are doing nothing. What we are in fact doing is what is outlined in this book, building sons who will become fathers, which requires sacrificial love, hard work, time, effort, patience, preparation, etc.

It requires someone to:

❖ Study the blueprint.

❖ Desire that pattern in his or her own life.

❖ Be obedient to follow the pattern

❖ Hunger to see the results it brings.

When this is our motivation for ministry, there will be longevity of results. If we want to see large and influential ministries impacting thousands and even millions of people, we first need to build a solid foundation. When that is established upon God's Word and empowered by the Spirit within the ministry of God Himself and set in place by a true son, then the ministry will progress to whatever level God has planned for it.

The challenge, though, is due to the nature of the contemporary church. It is very hard for any minister or leader to wait for long-term results. Everyone wants instant success and their ability is questioned by others when that is not the case. If people are not being saved all the time, something is wrong. But we must ask ourselves *what it is they are being saved into, made into the image of, and what will it look like in the end?* These pertinent questions are very important to the thinking minority. Of course we must trust in God and believe that the Spirit of God within the believer and follower of Christ will cause all these things to come to pass, but if the fullness of this life is to be lived upon the earth, there must be builders and there must be those who understand the blueprint and desire to see it come into fruition. We can then cooperate with the Holy Spirit submitting ourselves to His plan and working with Him in it.

We must learn to take the time necessary to disciple individual believers for the purpose of raising up sons so that they can become fathers who raise up sons like themselves. The heart of apostolic fathering is turned toward raising sons by being fathers who minister security, belonging, and identity.

> **Apostolic fathers minister security, belonging, and identity.**

When Jesus had fulfilled His mission and completed His task, it appeared to others that He had lost everything and everyone! There were no concrete buildings erected in His name, no huge congregation established; He seemed to upset most people in some way, and was rejected by the majority. *But,* He raised up sons after His own heart the whole time He was here. He planted seeds in the lives of men and women that were not yet visible.

When He shouted out, "It is finished," it was; but to those whom God the Father had given to Him, He had lost none. He had managed to bring them through; He had prepared the next generation who would reproduce in even greater measure.

We have biblical examples of those who, unlike Jesus, failed to raise up sons with a like heart. Elisha, who was fathered by Elijah, failed to raise up a son to continue all that the Lord had passed on to him. The double portion anointing on Elisha was never properly passed down to the next generation so that even when he was buried it was still trapped within his bones! (See Second Kings 13:20.) Sadly, David as well failed to raise up his own sons in God's proper order, which eventually led to the rebellion of Absalom.

A WORTHY PURSUIT

It's true that apostolic fathers bear a great deal of responsibility for the raising of sons; as with natural children, they also bear responsibility for the outworking of God's order in their lives. Although not all fathers are apostles, all apostles are to be fathers; and apostolic ministry encompasses the qualities of both the father and mother.

> *But we were gentle among you, just as a nursing mother cherishes her own children...we exhorted and comforted, and charged every one of you, as a father does his own children* (1 Thessalonians 2:7-11).

Although the hearts of the fathers must desire and be turned toward the children, the desire in the heart of a son is proven by his pursuit of the father. *Sons pursue fathers; fathers provide for their sons.*

Chapter Nine

WOMEN'S MINISTRY—PART OF HIS BLUEPRINT

Over the years I have read and heard much about the subject of women in ministry. Although there are a number of different stances on the topic, two compelling but opposite conclusions take center stage in these discussions. Briefly, one is sure that women *do not* belong in teaching and authority-based ministries in the church, and the other is certain that they *do* (with various restrictions or lack thereof). Both sides support their convictions with Scriptures.

My desire here is not to make theological arguments either against or in agreement with these stands. But, rather, I humbly submit the firm witness in my own heart concerning women in apostolic ministry as a result of understanding, which the Lord has given me over the years.

Although many authors choose to write their views without including the beliefs of their own hearts, I find it very difficult to hide my personal convictions behind an intriguing mass of theological points. Therefore, I am compelled to share what I believe to be true from my heart—convictions born out of the truth of ministry that I oversee, and for which I must one day give account.

Before the Lord found us we were lost, children of disobedience following the course of this world headed for destruction. Selfishness and pride was doing a complete job of stealing from us, and destroying us, although perhaps we were completely unaware of what was actually taking place! But in His great loving-kindness and mercy, He rescued us most wonderfully and completely.

God took out the stony, cold, hard heart and put within us a new heart. He recreated our spirit being and put within us His own Holy Spirit. With the help and leading of His Spirit, we begin to walk in a new way, treading the blueprint of life that He designed and created for us before the foundation of the world.

With this new heart came new love, having received the love of God poured out into our hearts by His Spirit. This love is the very same as the selfless love of God—always toward God and always toward others. This love is the foundation of all that God does and all that He is. His truth is established and founded in this love.

In examining the Word and seeking out His heart, we must always remember His great love. The Scripture says "speaking the truth in love"—that is the important thing. Perhaps sometimes we think we are speaking the truth, but if it is devoid of God's love, it is not founded in His love and flowing from His love.

Although we are addressing the question, *Can women be an apostolic gift and function in such a role within the church,* there is a crucial aspect I want to share that involves every man and woman.

To walk in His blueprint of life that God has designed and desires for us, and because this blueprint is founded and established love and comes from selflessness, *no one can truly experience it—not the unfolding, building, and impartation of it to others, or the submitting to it and receiving of it for oneself—outside of that love.*

You have received a new heart, a recreated spirit, and the Holy Spirit. The Holy Spirit is within you, and His love is poured out within you. This love is the very same love that God is, and His truth is founded and established in this selfless love.

THE S WORD—SUBMISSION

One of the great challenges in terms of anything to do with women in ministry is the issue of submission. A great deal of damage has been done in the name of this word. Over the course of history, the amount of abuse, hurt, control, and manipulation that has been justified under the heading of submission is immeasurable. For the most part, men have wanted women to submit to them believing that it leads to a much quieter and easier life…but does it?

Have we really understood the word submission in the light of God's love? I think not. Personally, I find the lack of understanding and hardness of hearts in the majority of church leaders on this topic to be quite distressing. In many cases, I believe we can hide behind the Word of God in misguided attempts to "keep women in their place."

In fervor to keep women "where they belong," as men we also can fail to realize, uphold, and honor the vital role God has given women in the training and influence of the generations. This role is apparent in the fact that the Father, in His infinite wisdom, deemed it right that for the first seven years of a child's life the mother would be the one with the greater influence. It is important in the shaping of generations that men see and protect the place God has given women in the home and the lives of children. Although she works together with the father, the mother is given the incredible task and ability to help form and nurture children for all that they will experience in the years to come. Mom is the one who sets the tone for their lives.

Sadly, not only is the role of wife and mom not encouraged and honored in today's society, but in the eyes of many it is actually despised. As a result, the vital, life-shaping role of mother is actually decreasing. The task of a mother giving herself to the raising of young children, which was once considered normal, is now becoming "abnormal."

Many biblical teachers who admonish women that their place is the home, at their husband's side, and looking after children, would use some of these same arguments for submission. Yet instead of bringing a new understanding and breathing life into the dying role of women raising children, their biblical rhetoric and heavy stance merely outline a job. More often than not they can belittle women's standing to a prescribed and legalistic sense of duty. Addressing the issue in this way doesn't really touch the underlying causes for why so many women, both inside and outside the church, are fighting for their real identity.

The church has been ruled by the heart of man far too long! Men have used God's Word to justify suppressing women—the Word without the breath of life or love in it. The result has been the ministry of death and condemnation to millions of our dear sisters in Christ, all in the name of a loving God. Because of this, the lessons we can learn from women's great capacity for love have, in many cases, been robbed from the church.

THEY LOVED HIM

A glimpse of the women at the cross reveals a beautiful biblical example of true love and commitment to Christ. Interestingly, as we look at the accounts of Jesus' followers at the time of the crucifixion, we see that all the disciples ran away, except the women and John the beloved. They did not despair, give in to fear, and run away like the majority of men did, even though they too were probably expecting Jesus to live, overcome the Romans, and usher in a new Kingdom on the earth with Jerusalem as its center.

I believe the women did not run because they had already given everything they had to follow Jesus; they had nothing left to lose and so had no reason to run away. In that culture and that time, they were something less in the eyes of men, so they weren't entertaining visions of grandeur. *They weren't expecting to be seated with Him ruling and reigning gloriously—they simply loved Him.*

The men seemed to be in love with themselves and all that they were expecting to be in the new Kingdom Jesus would set up. The disciples thought they still had a lot to lose. They still had themselves to die to—their dreams and visions, their positions ruling with Christ—and it all had to die before they could ever really enter into the true Kingdom of God.

The ones who got really close to Him, who really ministered to Him, were the women. They loved Him, they anointed Him, honored Him, provided for Him, and looked after Him in both life and death. In fact, a woman was the first one to see Jesus risen from the dead. She saw the angelic, interacted with the supernatural, and met with Jesus Himself after He rose from the grave. When Peter and John went to the tomb, they looked in, saw it empty, and went back home. I believe that this story raises some interesting questions. Questions that don't necessarily require an answer but that we would do well to think through—questions provoked by God's Word. When they were choosing a person to replace Judas as an apostle, the requirement was that this person would be a witness of His resurrection from the dead.

So, if Mary was the first to see Him, should she have been the one to take Judas' place as an apostle? Was it the cultural and theological mindset of the other apostles at the time that kept them from considering a woman for the position? Did they cast lots when they could have asked Jesus for the answer to the question of who would replace him? Are we too stuck in cultural and theological mindsets that keep us from perceiving the things that God wants to do with women in the church?

> **The women loved Jesus, looked after Him, and honored Him. They provided for Him both in life and in death.**

He Loved Them

The women loved Jesus, and Jesus loved these women in return, not for what they could do, but for who they were. He allowed them to be with Him, to follow Him, and to do all that they had in their hearts for Him. He never hindered or belittled them; He always encouraged them, released them and set them free.

> *Now it came to pass, afterward, that He went through every city and village, preaching and bringing the glad tidings of the kingdom of God. And the twelve were with Him, and certain women who had been healed of evil spirits and infirmities—Mary called Magdalene, out of whom had come seven demons, and Joanna the wife of Chuza, Herod's steward and Susanna, and many others who provided for Him from their substance* (Luke 8:1-3).

Jesus saw them in the light of the love of His Father, not in the constraints of a legalistic word that could be used to oppress and abuse them to make them do whatever men wanted—behavior that men would then use Scriptures to justify!

Of course, there is an order clearly set out by God in Scripture. Men and women do have differing roles and gifts, and God's Word does address the issue of headship and submission. But these can not be sorted out by our understanding of Scripture alone. The answer must be found in perceiving the Truth with a right heart.

HEARTS INFUSED WITH GOD'S LOVE

I realize that we are looking at "women in apostolic ministry," but before we can really get God's perspective on this issue, we must open our hearts that He might speak to us anew. *When Jesus was tempted by the devil He overcame not because He quoted the right Scripture, but because He had the right heart.* His heart was fully turned toward and submitted to the Father. All the authority, the power, the rule of His Sonship would be used for the sake of His Father, His Kingdom, and those whom the Father loved.

For us to see God's perspective on anything clearly we too must have a heart that desires His Kingdom to come and His will to be done above all else—a heart that is full of the love of God toward God, and also toward men and women, a heart like Christ's overflowing with love for His Bride, the Church.

As I have looked at Ephesians 5 concerning Christ and His love for the Church, I have had to think of myself as a "bride." This is not easy for a man. But yet Jesus, as a man, is speaking to the Church, as His Bride.

LOVING HIM AS OUR HUSBAND

I love Him because He has given His life so completely and totally for me. He has removed my old, disgusting clothes of a sinner, taken the stink of death away, and covered me in completely new and beautiful clothes of righteousness. He has spoken to me of His love, to change and transform me in many and wonderful ways. And He is not satisfied with just that, but He is also giving me a new future full of new dreams. He has a blueprint for my life; *I believe that I am worth* something and can be useful to someone. And the longer I live with Him, the more He desires to equip and release me into all that He has for me. My dreams are becoming reality, and I find that in Him I am becoming the person that He always desired and purposed for me to be. I am partaking of the adventure of serving Him, and the excitement never stops!

Jesus, the Husband of the Bride, loves us, sees us, thinks about us, and is always working toward bringing His desire for us to become a reality in our lives. This sort of love, in our hearts and His, is the mystery of Christ and the Church.

For Him, our hearts are the issue. With a new heart from the Father we can, like Jesus, move on with what He has for us. When our hearts are infused with the selfless love of God, we are willing to lay down our lives for others. This is the love of the husband for His church, this is the love that every husband should have for his wife. With this sort of love at the core, submission is not a difficult thing—it is a beautiful and safe thing.

And surely if this is His heart toward each one of us, who together make up His Bride, the Church, then this should be the heart of every man toward every woman. Less than this is not the heart of God, but rather the heart of man.

Jesus saw everyone in the light of the love of His Father, not in the constraints of a religious, legalistic word. The answer is found in perceiving the truth with a right heart. When Jesus was tempted by the devil, He overcame not because He quoted the Scripture but because He had a right heart.

> **Jesus saw everyone in the light of the love of His Father, not in the constraints of a religious, legalistic word.**

A wife who is loved like this, or a woman who finds a church like this, will experience the joy of a new sense of security, significance, and identity. Under these circumstances a woman can enjoy being a woman. She will no longer feel inferior, or less human, but will have a fresh sense of meaning and purpose. She will begin to understand that the blueprint Jesus lived is the same blueprint she can enjoy too—she will experience a new lease on life!

As this kind of love is poured out in a woman's heart, she can become all the Lord has purposed and desired her to be. *I believe this includes apostolic and prophetic ministry*; indeed, I believe it includes all of the fivefold gifts of God to the church.

A BEAUTIFUL EXPRESSION

In closing this topic, I share a lovely picture of God working apostolically through a woman from my personal experience. I presently have the privilege of serving and giving apostolic oversight to a church in Palermo, Italy. I find that it is one of the most beautiful expressions of the church that I have ever been honored to serve.

This church is special in many ways, but it is particularly unique in its leadership. Specifically, God has called a woman, Cristiana D'Amico, to provide apostolic ministry as head of this church. Her husband is very gifted and works alongside her, but it is Cristiana who has laid the foundation and has the wisdom to equip, release, and build the church into God's vision for it. She is also serving, through relationship, into other parts of Italy and the nation of Greece. There is no doubt that Cristiana is a true minister of the gospel with apostolic vision to build according to the pattern of the blueprint laid down by Christ.

It is clear to all three of us, Cristiana, Nunzio (her husband), and I, that she is the one whom God has chosen to walk in apostolic ministry, even though women ministers are generally not received in Italy. It has nothing to do with Nunzio being unwilling or disobedient. He stands with Cristiana in ministry and in many ways complements and supports the ministry, while also ministering himself.

The Lord Himself has placed us together. Cristiana is rightly submitted to me as an apostolic ministry, while also being submitted to her husband. This submission is not a negative thing, but rather a source of safety and security that results in greater freedom and liberty for Cristiana, fully releasing her to move in obedience to God.

I have often heard it said that when there is no man available, God calls a woman. Not only do I not believe this; I think it is a desperate ploy of the enemy to belittle the call of God in a women's life. It is one of the enemy's ways to hinder the flow of God's gifts and callings to the church through women.

For someone like Cristiana in a male-dominated society and culture, the cost can be amazingly difficult. However, we believe that God is doing a great work through His choice of Cristiana. We are not only lifting up the standard of the Lord, but the bastion of male dominance—a very strong principality—is actually being dealt with in this way to help set a whole nation free through the love of God.

Cristiana writes the following:

> As a father, apostle Paul [Hubbard] gives life to everything that is in God's heart for me and the church in Palermo; he protects it and makes it grow. The way he does this is by giving himself without seeking a personal interest, while I receive it and accept his teachings and instructions "not as the word of men, but as it actually is, the word of God" (1 Thessalonians 2:13 NIV).

> This submission of the heart is not in theory, but it applies to practical situations. How does this work? Paul comes over to visit every three months—he spends time with my family and with the church. Every time, I update him of what has gone on, every progress made, and every hard time that I or the church has been through. Then, I listen very carefully to any suggestion or instruction with the intention of putting it into practice faithfully, without judging, arguing, or doubting. During the whole process, I willingly decide to die to myself, because I have learned the spiritual principle that LIFE comes from death.

> When my submission and obedience are motivated and supported by my sincere faith (trust), the Kingdom is released and with it a greater anointing and maturity come. This is how I give God the opportunity to open new doors for me to preach His Word and help other ministers.

> I am aware of the fact that this is also the result of understanding the place God gave to my husband. Despite being a minister, at home I am wife and mother, according to God's order and I recognize my sphere of action and my husband's authority.

> —Cristiana D'Amico
> The Way of Holiness Church, Palermo, Italy

IT'S AMAZING

Over the years I have heard many and various "amazing" reasons why women cannot teach within the church or be involved in the ministry; none of them seem to me to be valid. Here are just a few examples:

❖ It's amazing that women can be teachers of infants, children, and young people, those in their most impressionable years, and yet cannot teach in the church.

❖ It's amazing that some of the same women who teach in schools, nurseries, youth clubs, Sunday schools, and most every sphere, agree with and uphold that they cannot teach or preach in the church.

❖ It's amazing that some leaders invite wives into their leadership meetings, but they are not allowed to share. On returning home, the husband shares with his wife who sees a new side of a situation shared earlier and then the husband promotes his wife's thoughts within the leadership—without telling anyone!

❖ It's amazing that some leaders don't invite their wives into their leadership meetings but do exactly as above!

❖ It's amazing that some would exhort their wives to wear a head covering to show their submissive hearts, but in truth that shows nothing of the sort. A submissive heart loves, respects, honors, and trusts—with or without a head covering.

❖ It's amazing that a man can trust his wife to nurture, care, and bring up his children, but does not trust her enough to share from the pulpit.

❖ It's amazing what men have done because of inadequate love and fear, and how that fear has caused a backlash of rebellion with disastrous consequences on the family.

❖ It's amazing to see how Scripture can be used aside from God's love and grace to bind up, break, destroy, and kill—that's what happens when the kind of selfless love, the God kind of love, is not found in our hearts and lives.

In the Kingdom of God there is and always will be equality, and yet there is and will also be rulership and headship, submission and accountability, authority, and respect. In the Kingdom there is also love, real, selfless, God-like love, and because of that love and the way that love is and behaves, all these strong and often difficult "examples" are experiential realities. But seriously considering all these words will bring forth good and beautiful things, they will not cause pain but will cause great joy and freedom.

As we release the love of God that is in our hearts and allow the Word of God that has been given to us to flow through us, we will release one another more and more into the wonderful blueprint that God has for each one us and for us together as the Church.

Women who are loved like this, in and through this selfless love , will find a new sense of freedom and joy. They will experience new adventure and feel valued. They will know this blueprint of life that Jesus has designed. They can be released into all the spheres that God has prepared, including apostolic ministry—building others according to His plan.

Chapter Ten

AUTHORITY FOR IMPLEMENTING THE BLUEPRINT

The whole of Second Corinthians 10 is about Paul's authority in the sphere that God had given him. As a master craftsman working together with God building the temple of both individuals and also of the church together, Paul was building according to the blueprint and the pattern given to Him by Christ. As with any master builder, authority needs to be exercised so that the building is built according to the blueprint.

Before I discuss Paul's apostolic authority, I would like to point out that only an apostolic people (or a people desiring to be built) will truly understand this subject. It will be easy to misinterpret what I am trying to say without a desire deep down in your heart.

As on every building site, sometimes the master builder has to exercise his authority to make sure that the building is built according to the blueprint. It is no different regarding our lives. For example, a number of years ago a young man in the church made up some stories about how ill he was and how he had been through some terrible traumatic events that had changed his life forever. Eventually, it came to light that he had been compulsively lying about these things. All the while, though, the church had been in fervent prayer.

The young man had to repent of his deception and I asked him to stand before the church and tell the congregation the whole truth. My request was made in great meekness, while honoring my authority in the Lord. When his sincere repentance took place, a "great fear" fell upon the whole church and the presence of the Lord was greatly revered.

Paul himself has the boldness to declare his God-given authority. For instance, "...about our authority which the Lord gave us for edification and not for your destruction, I shall not be ashamed" (2 Cor. 10:8). This verse makes it clear that Paul understood apostolic authority could be wielded for building up and for tearing down.

In Second Corinthians 10:10, we see that the vessel carrying this powerful authority cannot necessarily be identified by appearance, "For his letters," they say, "are weighty and powerful, but his bodily presence is weak, and his speech contemptible." Paul goes on to say, that in the Corinthian church, there was a problem with people looking at and measuring one another by outward appearance and expression. They were "...measuring themselves by themselves, and comparing themselves among themselves..." (2 Cor. 10:12).

Hence, a great speaker who was very charismatic dressed in the latest Italian designer suit and looking the part would become the standard by whom everyone else with authority in the church would measure themselves. They would then commend themselves to one another—this Paul refused to do! Paul understood God-appointed spheres of authority, and he knew which spheres were his. This is evident from Second Corinthians 10:13, "We, however, will not boast beyond measure, but within the limits of the sphere which God appointed us—a sphere, which especially includes you." Like Paul, it is also important for us to be faithful within our sphere.

WITHIN OUR SPHERE

Paul goes on to show how his authority works, and the effect it has within the spheres God has appointed him. He makes it clear that a sphere of influence always includes people. Without people following, a leader is disqualified. Simply put, *you can't be called a leader if no one will follow your lead.*

Each of us has been given a sphere, or spheres, in which God has called us to help further His Kingdom on the earth. Like Paul, within each of these spheres we are called to exercise the abilities God has given us with faith, wisdom, authority, and leadership.

In Second Corinthians 10:14 we read, "for we are not overextending ourselves (as though our authority did not extend to you)…for it was to you that we came with the gospel of Christ." God had given Paul something to deliver to the people in Corinth. If He hadn't done that he would have no right to work in that sphere. It is also interesting to note that even Paul did not overextend himself outside the sphere God had given him.

We are overextending ourselves when we take credit for things that we have not done, when we attribute something to ourselves that is done outside our God-given sphere in a place where we have no authority. We may well desire the right to speak into people's lives. But if we have not labored unto delivery something God has given us for that sphere, then we have no authority to do so unless invited by the one whom God has called to work that field. (They are free to invite whosoever they desire.)

Paul makes it clear that he is, "not boasting of things beyond measure, that is in other men's labors…" (2 Cor. 10:15). It is easy to boast in other men's labors, but the true measure of our fruit is seen in our own labor, and in the lives over which God has given us oversight. In other words, the places in which God has given us authority are easy to identify by the fruit that is manifest in the lives of the people there. The result of faithfulness in our sphere(s) is that the people under us will experience change and increase in their individual lives. And the effects of this for those who rightly exercise their God-given authority, is that their field will be enlarged. "…but having hope, that as your faith is increased, we shall be greatly enlarged by you in our sphere" (2 Cor. 10:15).

I want to make it clear that this does not mean that Paul took control of people's lives. He knew that simply living in the fullness of life He had received from God would result in an increase of faith for the people to whom he ministered. In turn, as they were equipped by receiving what he delivered to them and their faith increased, the field that Paul was working in would be enlarged. The influence of God's life flowing through him would touch more and more people.

As Paul faithfully invested what God had given him into people's lives, it had the automatic affect of increase in his own life—in his present spheres of influence and the addition of new ones. Therefore, he did not have to concern himself with commending himself to others, looking for the next ministry opportunity, or opening doors to walk through. His sphere of authority and influence was automatically enlarged "to preach the gospel in the regions beyond you..." (2 Cor. 10:16).

GOING BEYOND

Many of us who believe in Jesus are also interested in going beyond. Many believers want to go to the next level or dimension, but this can only happen as we are faithful in what the Lord has already given us. Paul's faithfulness in his personal walk with God, in his present sphere, and his right use of authority, broke open regions "beyond" for his influence.

Fathers of the faith who have gone before us and accomplished great things in God have followed this same pattern of faithfulness. Looking at their examples often stirs in us a desire to go beyond in our own lives. But *what they have done is their accomplishment, not ours.* If we want to experience accomplishments like them, we must also be faithful in the sphere God has already assigned to us.

The way to be faithful in our given sphere is to walk in the Spirit. This means that we exhibit the fruit of God's Spirit in our nature. Like Christ, we choose to consistently walk in love, joy, peace, patience, kindness, meekness, and self-control. When we live and move in His Spirit, then we become mighty men and women of God who walk in the realm of His Kingdom in our everyday lives. Not in a superior realm, but a spiritual realm. In this place there is powerful authority, which has its basis in the very life of God, and is always motivated by the love of God.

This is a place where the enemy cannot stand, speak, walk, or even look into—there is nothing in him that belongs here! When we choose to walk in this realm by walking in the *life of God, not only are we able to minister mending, equipping and healing but we are also able to pull down strongholds.*

PULLING DOWN STRONGHOLDS

We can go through the motions of spending hours in prayer believing we are pulling down strongholds, binding and loosing an endless number of "spirits" in heavenly places, spend time shouting and saying the "right things," but in the end, if you are not walking in the Spirit, it all means nothing! In Second Corinthians 10:4-5, Paul says that his weapons are, "pulling down strongholds, casting down arguments and every high thing that exalts itself against the knowledge of God...." So we see that he was not only addressing very difficult situations, into which he was able to bring healing and necessary equipping, but beyond that, he was pulling down strongholds and every high thing that was seeking to exalt itself against God.

Paul was able to deal with arguments and every high thing that had raised itself up in people's minds, and bring them into captivity to God. As he pulled down strongholds of wrong thinking, he was able to introduce a new way of thinking, replacing strongholds with thoughts that were based on God's Word and obedience to Christ. Paul was aware that the authority he carried to accomplish this change in thinking was most powerful when clothed in meekness. Through the meekness and gentleness flowing from the deep well of life that Paul made a habit of living in the Spirit, he was able to address strongholds that had kept God's people captive. He knew that he carried a weight of authority, which could either build up or break down.

Build Up or Break Down

After Paul tore down strongholds and established their thoughts in obedience to Christ, Second Corinthians 10:6 tells us that he was then, "...ready to punish all disobedience when your obedience is fulfilled." In other words, it was then expected that the people of God would begin to be and do all that had been revealed; and if they did not, it seems that there would be punishment. I realize that most of us do not like to hear about that! But it is in the Word and so should not be ignored. Obviously Paul preferred, "...pleading...by the meekness and gentleness of Christ" (2 Cor. 10:1).

Paul did not rejoice in opportunities to correct the church. He said in verse 2, "But I beg you that when I am present I may not be bold with that confidence by which I intend to be bold against some *who think of us as if we walked according to the flesh.*" This is the underlying problem: when people look, they see according to the flesh, and do not see or understand what is taking place in the Spirit, "Do you look at things according to the outward appearance?" (2 Cor. 10:7).

When Paul was not present with them, he felt the need to speak strongly and clearly, emphasizing the real issues of people's souls, in order to reach beyond appearances into people's hearts. As a result, his written communication was much more forceful and bold than when he communicated with them in person. He did not want to be as bold when he was bodily present as he was when he wrote to them, because he knew the weight of the authority he carried; he preferred to come in gentleness and meekness. Therefore, he writes, "But I will come to you shortly, if the Lord wills, and I will know, not the word of those who are puffed up, but the power. For the Kingdom of God is not in word but in power. What do you want? Shall I come to you with a rod, or in love and a spirit of gentleness" (1 Cor. 4:19-21). Paul begged that it could be the latter.

The challenge for Paul then, was that when he did come bodily, in meekness and gentleness, the people thought he was a wimp and didn't give his words the weight they deserved. They knew he was bold and spoke strongly when he wrote, but when he was with them, he tended to be more tender, and they misread this as weakness, as though he were walking by the flesh, and they judged him as such, "For though we walk in the flesh, we do not war according to the flesh. For the weapons of our warfare are not carnal..." (2 Cor. 10:3-4). What weapons were they? Well, I think not the usual weapons we hear many Bible teachers speak of (in Eph. 6), the armory is not the weaponry; armory is what protects us! Weaponry is what we use to destroy and demolish the enemy.

DESTROY AND DEMOLISH

What is this weaponry then? What is it that the enemy cannot approach? What is the thing he cannot face, and that he fears the most? Paul tells us that this weapon is not according to the flesh, but that it is "mighty in God." It is when the Spirit of the Lord is upon us; when we, like Jesus are, *anointed to* preach good tidings to the poor...heal the brokenhearted...proclaim liberty to the captives, and the opening of prison to those who are bound (see Isa. 61:1).

Even though Paul walked in the Spirit and was clearly equipped with this weapon, he was often misunderstood. To address many of the problems and challenges he faced, he had to use strong and forceful words in an attempt to bring discipline and order. This was necessary for him to establish God's plumb line, His measure of righteousness in the church, and was something that Paul was anointed to do. He was also bringing forth a revelation of Christ that was beyond what had so far been revealed to those around him, things that might not be immediately accepted and understood "...as also our beloved brother Paul, according to the wisdom given him, has written to you, as also in all his epistles, speaking in them of these things, in which are some hard things to understand, which untaught and unstable people twist to their own destruction, as they do also the rest of the Scriptures" (2 Peter 3:15-16).

Even though Paul often had to address situations forcefully, the truth about Paul was that he was a very meek and gentle man. In fact, this meekness was the foundation for the strength of his authority in the Spirit. Numbers 12:3 speaks of another very meek man with great authority, Moses. And in Matthew 11:29 we read that Jesus was, "gentle and lowly in heart." When Paul was face to face with the beloved of the Lord, he was overcome by His meekness and gentleness.

Meekness and Gentleness

This apostle Paul who said ...*in presence am lowly among you, but being absent and bold toward you...* Why would this be? Because of the love of God for His people.

The way to be faithful in our God-given spheres is by walking in the Spirit. Choose consistently to walk in love, joy, peace, patience, kindness, meekness, and gentleness. In this place there is powerful authority that has its basis in the very life of God. Authority is most powerful when clothed in meekness. Remember, building according to the blueprint requires authority to be exercised.

Many times prior to addressing a situation personally, my spirit will be moved, grieved, pained, and even sometimes angered by what has been going on. But always I ask the Lord that I might minister in meekness and gentleness, knowing that each one involved is His special treasure, His beloved sheep. I have come to understand that for whatever reason, when I am present to address a difficult situation where there have been tensions and challenges and people are upset, it's as though the balm of the Spirit arrives. Then, as I speak and minister into the situation, the Lord gently yet powerfully works. In the end, I know that I am not able to glory in anything that I have done, but *I am free to glory in the Lord.*

GLORY IN THE LORD

It is the same for each one of us as we move faithfully within the sphere that God has given us. When we use all that God has deposited in us, and exercise the authority He has given us in meekness and gentleness, then we see that "it is good," and we can boast in the Lord—always knowing that it is through Him and in Him that we have accomplished the things He has put before us. "For he who commends himself is not approved, but whom the Lord commends" (2 Cor. 10:18).

In conclusion, for us to enjoy the fullness of life, we must receive apostolic authority into our lives so that we will be built in accordance with His blueprint and plan. We can also know if we are apostolically approved by testing ourselves against the Word of God in Second Corinthians 10. If we are ministering in the sphere God has given us, walking in the Spirit of the Lord, and exhibiting the meekness and gentleness of the love of God to all, then perhaps we are beginning to walk in the blueprint of life. Perhaps we are becoming a truly apostolic people of God upon the earth.

Chapter Eleven

APOSTOLIC FINANCES

The heart of apostolic finance is not about making money. Neither is it about having the things we need or being prosperous and successful, although it may include those things. *It is* centered in Christ; it's all about Jesus and His Kingdom and using all that we have for Kingdom purpose.

> *Seek ye first the Kingdom of God and His righteousness, and all these things will be added to you* (Matthew 6:33).

Of course His blueprint for our lives includes promises that He has made to us for everything pertaining to life and godliness. So there is nothing that we need that He hasn't made available and hasn't already provided for us in Jesus.

If the church is ever again going to find the place as in the Book of Acts, "nor was there anyone among them who lacked," we must come to a new understanding about finances (see Acts 4:34). Our finances must be brought into the Kingdom realm by centering them on Christ. Sadly, this has not been the case in many Christian circles.

KINGDOM VISION

In recent years, the Western church in particular has become consumed with prosperity and success. Much of that message focuses on how we can become better off materialistically. Now, this idea is not in itself a wrong one. However, when it becomes the motivation for life, and our vision and goals are centered on prospering and doing better financially, that is a problem. When we make money our focus, we will never truly be happy or satisfied deep in our inner spirit. How could we be when that is not what we were created for?

We were created by the Father to know Him and to have an intimate relationship with Him, including the assurance of spending eternity with Him. *Anything less than intimacy with God will never be enough to satisfy our souls.*

The blueprint for life is not about making money, although we may make money and have more than enough. It is about living life to the full with the Father and having adventures in His Spirit, bringing glory to Him.

Unfortunately, some believers have lowered their sights; they have embraced an earthly vision focused on fulfilling goals that are of an earthly nature. But when we look carefully at the original disciples, like the apostle Paul, we see that their vision was not about obtaining things, it was all about a Man, Jesus. Paul's vision centered on the Kingdom of God, and the goals that Jesus gave him were all of a spiritual nature. In his lifetime Paul had the joy of being able, by God's grace, to say that he had accomplished his Kingdom goals! God has goals for us that come with the grace to see them through, so that we, too, can know this joy.

As believers we should not be living by the light of an earthly vision. The truth is that living by the Word gives us wisdom to see and embrace real Kingdom vision. Fulfilling this heavenly blue print for life. In the wake of living by God's wisdom comes all that a man or woman of God could desire. It is when you and I choose to seek first His Kingdom that all these other things (that people are chasing after) will chase after us! *When we give our all for Jesus, He will give His all for us.* Doing it Jesus way, according to His heart and His Kingdom, results in life and health, and everything that we could possibly need.

> **The blueprint of life includes promises of God pertaining to life and godliness, including wealth.**

Ruled by His Word

To truly enter into the realm of apostolic finances, it is vital that our hearts are right. A heart that is totally surrendered to the King and His Kingdom and ruled by His Word and wisdom is a necessity. When we are utterly in love with Jesus, then we are among those whom He will cause to inherit wealth. God's wisdom says, "I love those who love me, and those who seek me diligently will find me. Riches and honor are with me, enduring riches and righteousness. My fruit is better than gold, yes, than fine gold, and my revenue than choice silver. I traverse the way of righteousness in the midst of the paths of justice, that I may cause those who love me to inherit wealth, *that I may fill their treasuries*" (see Prov. 8:17-21).

If, rather than being taken up with how to be successful by making more money and learning the latest ten steps to prosperity, we would give ourselves entirely over to Him, then *we might find great treasures pursuing us!*

Kingdom Mindset

It is true that there's a great deal written in the New Testament concerning finances. However, I believe that the instruction God gives us has more to do with our heart attitude than following methods to obtain His blessing. I have seen this worked out in various apostolic ministries that I am acquainted with, both near and far. None of them follow the same pattern, rather they have had something of God's heart revealed to them and sought to honor Him according to who He is. I have noticed that one of the most important aspects in looking at apostolic finances is not in how well we follow certain patterns, but in regard to the way we think. This is because apostolic ministry is not concerned with getting certain things and being successful in the world's eyes, but with transformation, with being conformed to the image of Christ (see Rom. 8:29 and 12:2).

Let me make it clear that God's Word says that the Lord wants us to be prosperous in every area of our lives. Third John 2 says, "Beloved I pray that you may prosper in all things and be in health, just as your soul prospers." Sadly, though, many become so fixated on this point that they no longer see the Kingdom. *But the key to realizing prosperity in every area of our lives is in the way we think.*

Many people limit their own possibilities and potential because they "think poverty." In other words, they have a small and negative mindset. For Christians, I believe this sort of thinking is a natural result of a sinner-unrighteous mentality. When we continually think of ourselves as unrighteous sinners, instead of the righteous of God in Christ Jesus, a highway of wrong thought patterns is set in cement in our brains. As we continually embrace this wrong mindset, the enemy of our souls eventually sees this pattern and dispatches an actual spirit of poverty to steal, kill, and destroy us. We can clearly see this in God's Word by looking at John 12 and the drama that unfolded during the celebration in Jesus' honor after He raised Lazarus from the dead.

Poverty Mindset

In John 12:1 we read, "Then, six days before the Passover, Jesus came to Bethany, where Lazarus was who had been dead, whom He had raised from the dead." Bethany means the house of poverty. Though this may seem an unlikely location for extravagant blessing, it is exactly where the Father brought the son to throw a party and bless Him lavishly! The Father wants to bless every child of His who is totally given over to His Kingdom purposes. He appoints special times of His lavish abundance for those He loves. In this case, He chose to do it right in the midst of poverty and that always causes a reaction, which exposes the poverty mentality and the spirits behind it. Here He used the act of a humble woman to expose the hearts around Him.

> *There they made Him a supper; and Martha served, but Lazarus was one of those who sat at the table with Him. Then Mary took a pound of very costly oil of spikenard, anointed the feet of Jesus, and wiped His feet with her hair. And the house was filled with the fragrance of the oil* (John 12:2-3).

Mary loved Jesus very much and wanted to honor Him not only with her words, but also with her substance. This oil of spikenard was lover's oil. It was very costly. She didn't need anyone's permission to do what she did, the oil was hers alone and she gave it from a heart of love. Yet this expression of sacrificial love caused an absolute uproar from the people around her. In light of her behavior, everything that goes with the poverty mentality—small mindedness, judgment, and condemnation—was exposed. The spirit of poverty became apparent when several of the group reacted by criticizing her sharply, including Judas, who was stealing from the funds.

> *But one of His disciples, Judas Iscariot, Simon's son, who would betray Him, said, why was this fragrant oil not sold for three hundred denarii and given to the poor? But there were some who were indignant among themselves, and said, why was this fragrant oil wasted? And they criticised her sharply* (see John 12:4-5 and Mark 14:3-5).

THE LIGHT OF LOVE

In light of Mary's expression of love for Jesus, we see the reaction of two completely opposed mindsets. One was taken up with loving Jesus, ministering to His needs, and the needs of the coming Kingdom. The other was continually looking at money, wanting more—even under the guise of being a good steward and wanting the money for the poor. That's what a spirit of poverty sounds like. Those bound by it cover their steps with religious talk, always being prudent and wise, never wanting to give too much. But God's good stewardship does not look anything like man's good stewardship!

The Father always wants to bless His children; those who are totally given over to Him He will bless abundantly. Lavish abundance exposes a mindset and spirit of poverty.

Man's idea of good stewardship is usually ruled by his own thoughts of what abundance is. His measuring line starts at poverty, or not enough, and ends up at maybe enough. So when he tempers it with fleshly wisdom and good judgment, he still ends up on the small side. He is always being watchful, and careful, but never entering into the real abundance of God. His small-mindedness limits everything he does. *God's measuring line is very different from men's. It starts with more than enough and ends in more than enough.* When God tempers His blessing with His wisdom, it is so we don't die of His overwhelming goodness and love!

If the poverty mindset is not identified for what it is, eventually a spirit inhabits it and begins to kill off everything that is good, beautiful, and lovely. When Judas intervened with his "good" stewardship and worldly ways, he put a stop to the incredible flow of life that they were all experiencing at that moment. A spirit of heaviness no doubt, entered into the house, and began working with poverty to steal away the life, the sense of worship and adoration, the blessing and sheer bliss of being with Jesus. Not only was his heart and the spirit in him exposed, but he also drew out of others what was in them. As they were affected by the words that exposed his poverty mindset, their own hearts and minds were exposed, "...out of the abundance of the heart the mouth speaks" (see Matt. 12:34).

In John 12:6, Judas' true motives are exposed, "This he said, not that he cared for the poor, but because he was a thief, and had the money box and he used to take what was put in it."

God's measuring line starts with more than enough and ends with more than enough.

> **Poverty steals everything, not just financial blessing.**

CHOSEN BY JESUS

A thief was at work on the inside of Judas. It could have come about for many reasons. Perhaps these wrong thoughts were birthed in his mind many years earlier. Maybe he was surrounded by wrong thinking as a child. Maybe he had experienced all sorts of challenges and hurts that we know nothing about. But greater than any struggles, handicaps, or life experiences he may have had, was the fact that he was chosen by Jesus. The Lord knew that if Judas wanted to, he could have made the right choices that would have enabled him to triumph over everything else and to become a true apostle.

Each disciple chosen by Him had the same opportunities. Each one of them had the same Master and Teacher. Each one was exposed to the same anointing and Word. *Eleven of them became apostles; one of them became a traitor.*

Poverty can steal from us because of the past. But greater than your past is the presence of Him who lives in you now. He redeems your past and enables you by His Spirit within to make good and right choices that will help you overcome.

It was because of a difference in their hearts that the others remained true. Judas' heart was not focused on Jesus and surrendered totally to Him, even though he was with Jesus every day, and life in all its fullness with everything that was good and wonderful was constantly available to him for over three years. Joy was surrounding him on every side as Jesus ministered to hurting people. Judas was unable to receive or enjoy any of it because he was focused in heart and mind upon *himself, his* needs, and what *he* wanted. A thief was stealing from him, and in turn he was stealing from others. The poverty mentality, coupled with the spirit of poverty, took such a hold upon Judas that everything was stolen from him, even his life.

THE KEY TO FREEDOM

You may be thinking that I am making too big a deal of all this, but you need to realize that a mentality of poverty and a spirit working within is a very dangerous and terrible thing. The enemy will not stop until his goal is reached—total ruin, complete destruction. You cannot afford to allow him any access, and you must be serious in your desire to stop him!

Simply identifying this thinking and spirit at work within is not enough. You must *identify* it, *confess* it as sin, and *repent* of it. Repentance, of course, means not just saying you are sorry, but doing the opposite of what you have been doing. This depth of change can only happen by the Spirit of God within you as you depend upon His Word.

> **You cannot live in the blueprint of life if poverty is stealing from you.**

Freedom does not come by simply asking someone to pray for us, though many would like it to be that simple. We move toward freedom from this terrible spirit only by radical means as we act and live in the opposite spirit. Freedom comes when we stop justifying our *smallness* of mind, and what we think is *good* stewardship and *wise* ways, and begin to do what we know we should in terms of our finances. That is just the beginning; after we take this step in our thinking, we must take action. The key to freedom is breakthrough in terms of our giving. Release comes when we begin to press into new dimensions in terms of giving and sowing.

As we learn to put first things first, giving to God what is His, and honoring Him with our substance we will naturally begin to do the things we should with our finances—things like looking after the poor and needy, and sowing into Kingdom endeavors. Then, when we are ready to give sacrificially, we can ask in faith for God to enlarge us to sow into His purposes above and beyond anything we have previously experienced.

New Highways

Only when we have *changed our way of thinking to line up with His Word, and changed our habits of living to line up with His character,* can we put to death the sin that so easily entangles us. The highways in our minds become new ones that take us on the way of God's goodness, grace, and righteousness, places where the provision of His abundance can flow in and through our lives. Then life becomes full of possibilities. Our small negative mindset changes, and we begin to enjoy God's perspective, seeing the things we *can* do for His Kingdom.

Over the years I have had many people who were interested in telling me what *cannot* be done. One of my favorite sayings:

> Don't tell me what we don't have, where we can't go, or what we can't do; instead tell me what we do have, where we can go, and what we can do!

I have learned that unless people are willing to do what has been written, according to the pattern that Jesus has set, they will never be used by the Lord to do anything that is above and beyond.

We must learn to see the possibilities of what we can do with what we have already been given—like the little boy with his lunch (see John 6). There must have been others there who had food with them. But only this little boy could see that Jesus could do something with what he had and was willing to give it to Him. Otherwise, we undermine ourselves and negate the great possibilities that God has for us.

Often those who suffer from a poverty mindset make decisions based on saving money, thinking that they are being good stewards. But we must remember that good stewardship in God's Kingdom comes from a place of immeasurable supply. *We should be more concerned about saving* **time** *than money.* Time can never be regained; it is more precious than anything. Those who see time as their most precious resource will make everything else work so that their time is fruitful. When we use money, for good or bad, it can always be made again, but not so with time. Money should be a servant to our time, not the other way around.

When God speaks to us about good stewardship, it is to people who have been made new creations, not old people with old thinking. He takes it for granted that we have the right priorities; that we are His children who have the love of God poured into us by His Spirit, that *we have new hearts within in us that delight and desire to bless and be generous, like His own.*

WHERE TO START

A good place to start with our giving is with tithing. Tithing is an initial heart response to the goodness of God, and a way in which we can honor Him for the goodness and abundance He has bestowed upon us (see Gen. 14:18-24). Although tithing is an Old Testament practice, it was established *before* the law. Tithing also shows us, particularly in the Old Testament, that God requires that our finances are ordered in a righteous way.

Although we know that in the New Testament we do not do things by the law, we fulfill the law of God in our hearts by His Spirit who lives in us. Yet, we can still learn from the law of God about His priorities and order in the area of finance. We can look to Old Testament types to help us learn what is pleasing to Him. In this case, we can learn several things from the practice of tithing in the Old Testament.

One is that as we give to God, He then takes from that and distributes it to those who minister before His altar and to His house, including the poor and needy among us. He also uses it to set the stones in

order and release them, thereby building His church in a way that releases the glory of God in His temple. Tithing is the simplest place to
begin learning to please and honor God with our finances.

God takes for granted that we have the right priorities. He has given
us a new heart, a new spirit, and the Holy Spirit within. We no longer
need the law of the old, because the new heart and the Spirit of God
have made us new. Now we want to please God because we love Him.

Chapter Twelve

APOSTOLIC FINANCES (CONTINUED)

It's only when we get to the heart of Christianity, and remain there, that we are able to talk about finances from the right perspective. The *only* perspective from which we can truly understand kingdom finance is when we view it from the heart of Christianity—the heart of love. Whenever Jesus spoke on the subject of finance, it was always from His heart. He did not give a one-to-ten point summary of how to prosper. Please understand me, I do not mean that we cannot give helpful points and principles on how to handle money. However, *teaching on finance should always be founded on and inspired by the right motivation and heart attitude.*

A MATTER OF THE HEART

In the Gospels we see a beautiful example in the story of Mary, the sister of Martha, who poured out a *pound of very costly oil of spikenard, and anointed the feet of Jesus.* This was an expression from her heart to the One she loved in response to all that He had done for her. This very costly offering was as nothing to her. In fact, it was the least she could do!

His involvement in her life had brought about huge change. Jesus transformed her through His Word. Mary had learned about Him, His Kingdom, and her Father in Heaven. As a result, she gained a whole wonderful, new perspective and outlook on life as she saw herself in the light of His love.

Mary understood that Jesus was preparing to sacrifice His life. She saw that He was doing this in order to make a way for the love of the Father and the reality of His Kingdom to come into her life. He was continually unfolding a blueprint for her life, and she was walking in it. It is possible that of all the disciples and followers of Jesus, she is the only one who really understood what He was actually doing, and what He would do, so that they could experience the fullness of His Kingdom.

This is why Jesus rebuked the disciples and said, "Let her alone; she has kept this for the day of My burial. For the poor you have with you always, but Me you do not have always" (John 12:7-8). Jesus' words make it clear that she had caught a glimpse of what He would have to do, and how much He would have to give, the tremendous cost of living real Kingdom life—the giving up of oneself in love for another. Jesus was giving up His life and Mary, in like manner, had no difficulty in giving up what was very costly to her to pour it on His feet. *This is where the root of apostolic finance is found; it's a **heart** thing.*

When someone gives up life for you, you want to give up your life for him. Finance is the least of everything—not the most.

Apart from the right motivation, money can corrupt and cause many sorrows. If we don't have love in our hearts for Jesus and the Kingdom, we will find other interests and outlets. Instead of loving Jesus, we might find ourselves loving money; and the love of money causes much evil. It's not the money itself, it's the heart that decides what will do us good, and what will cause us hurt and bring sorrow. This is why we must watch over our hearts and guard them with all diligence. "Keep your heart with all diligence, for out of it spring the issues of life" (Prov. 4:23).

As believers, we know that when we are born again we are made new. Our hearts and our spirits are touched and filled by the Holy Spirit. The Teacher, the Guide, the Lover comes to dwell within us. The very DNA of God is imparted to us. We partake of His divine nature through His promises. "Naturally" we then begin to think like Him, walk like Him, and talk like Him as we partake of His nature.

The very essence of God is to give, and He can do nothing other than love. It's who He is and always will be. He cannot help Himself;

He is always thinking and moving toward us in His love. He doesn't even think about it other than to order the way in which He does it.

If this is how God is, then as we become more like Him, it's how we are. We, too, love to give. It is not second nature, *it is our new God-given nature.* Some may say, "Yes, but surely we have to fight to overcome our selfishness?" Yes, we have a constant battle to overcome; however, we must begin to believe *that greater is He who is within us than he who is in the world.*

The Least of Things

In the Kingdom, the least of all things is financial, "He who is faithful in what is least is faithful also in much; and he who is unjust in what is least is unjust also in much" (Luke 16:10). Jesus goes on to make it clear what He is actually referring to, "Therefore if you have not been faithful in the unrighteous mammon, who will commit to your trust the true riches? And if you have not been faithful in what is another man's, who will give you what is your own?" (Luke 16:11-12).

There can be no doubt that Jesus is talking about finance. This is the least in terms of the Kingdom; finance is the currency of the world, faith is the currency of Heaven. There is no doubt that in order to enjoy the inheritance that the Father has given to us in Jesus' name, which is the nations, we need to see a great release of finance on the earth. *This release will only come through faith working by love,* and apostolic ministry is a key to us taking on the loving nature of our heavenly Father.

> **Great release of finance only comes through faith working by love.**

Apostolic ministry is always at work in the area of a person's heart and spirit to build up, transform, and restore. This is what the blueprint requires, that we are made according to His image, that we become more like Him. Every master craftsman is concerned about the building of the house becoming what the blueprint has decreed. God is constantly working to conform us to His image—transforming our minds and bringing them into line with His heart and will. When we become expressions of His love on earth, people will respond as they are touched by His love. However, we should be aware that when we give like God, the responses may not always look good to others.

When Mary poured out her costly ointment, there was uproar. Prior to this point they were enjoying a wonderful celebration in the presence of Jesus with the overflowing abundance of God, and sweet fellowship over a meal. They were having a wonderful time when Mary caused upheaval as her gift exposed the hearts of those around her.

GIVING WITH LOVE

Finances always expose the heart. They bring out what is deep within. Where nothing else can, the mention or use of money always does! *That's because if you love money, you can't let it go. But if you love Him, letting it go is easy.* It's interesting to note that the people gathered with Jesus discussed a matter that had nothing to do with them. It was not their perfume. It was not theirs to give or to keep. It was not theirs to pour out. This was an intimate time of sharing and fellowship between Jesus and Mary, two people who knew how to give the love of their hearts to each other.

It always amazes me that despite the fact Christians all over the world know that when they give they are giving *to Him*, many still want to have a say about where it goes, how it is used, who can use it, etc. This is *not* the same as giving with love. This scene of Judas and the disciples is a good case in point—they were all involved in the discussion. This same scenario plays out again and again all over the world in many different settings.

HARBORING THE WRONG SPIRIT

As previously stated, the same spirit that was at work in Judas, the spirit of poverty, has managed to find a place of refuge in some Christian minds. We do not need to harbor this wrong spirit. Judas was in bondage to wrong thinking where money was concerned only because he refused to be changed by the Spirit and Word of God. When we refuse to allow change in our lives by His Word and Spirit, over many years of patience and grace being poured out upon us, then the spirit of poverty comes looking for somewhere to live and finds it in minds that will not change. When we go that route, we cover it with nice-sounding arguments that have the appearance of wisdom, but have nothing at all to do with the Father's heart or His kingdom.

Like Judas, people may ask questions like, "Why was this fragrant oil not sold for three hundred denarii and given to the poor?" (John 12:5). Such people can cause great disruption and destruction in the house of God making a way for the spirit of poverty to continue affecting more people in the same way. Sadly, although we may think that it only involves finance, that is merely the place it starts. The truth is, that it can end with the total stealing of all life, "This he said, not that he cared for the poor, but because he was a thief [and had a thief working on the inside of him], and had the money box; and he used to take what was put in it" (John 12:6).

Judas had every opportunity to be changed and transformed, but he ended up committing suicide. He heard the Word, saw the Word, experienced fellowship with the Word, and saw all that Jesus did, yet he chose to continue in his old way and mindset. The Father loved him all the way, but Judas refused salvation.

Good and Wise Stewards

Judas was the steward of the great Apostle's purse, and no doubt his statement was welcomed by a number of the disciples as being prudent and wise, "but there were some who were indignant among themselves. ...And they criticized her sharply" (Mark 14:4-5). I can imagine that they were in agreement with what *seemed* to be a sensible and logical argument, but they were not operating in the Holy Spirit.

As Christians we are to become like Him, not the other way around. We are not trying to make Him as we are, causing Him to agree with our thinking and perspective. We can only be like the Master as we get to know Him. When we know how He thinks, how He sees things, and how He loves, then we will know that in Him is no lack. He has never been in need. He never even thinks lack. He is aware of it, but it is entirely alien to Him. He obviously sees the suffering and the pain that comes from it, *but He responds to faith working through love.*

Jesus was never poor! Indeed, when He was born, He was given very costly and precious gifts: gold, frankincense, and myrrh. His clothing was the latest "Armani," sewn as one piece. Many people provided for Him from their substance, and they had sufficient funds in the apostolic bag to take care of all the needs of Jesus and His disciples.

THE RIGHT MEASURE

Jesus always thinks abundance, prosperity, joy, generosity—it's His nature. It's who He is. Until we begin to think like He thinks, we will get the measure wrong. We may think that we are being abundant and generous when our abundance comes from a measure that has at one end lack and at the other abundance. Or perhaps we find ourselves in the middle at "just the right" place, but the measure of God starts and ends in abundance. It has no place or marker called lack. Of course, He has to use His wisdom so we are not overwhelmed with His goodness. The goodness of God could actually kill us in our present state. I believe that we need to go through something like the "valley of the shadow" just before we enter His presence, so we have a moment to adjust to His glorious presence and all that surrounds Him, before we see Him as He is.

There are many so-called wise stewards within the Christian church. They pride themselves on their prudence and care. However, it would be truly wise for every local church to be sure that their "wise stewards" are those who truly know Him, are being transformed through His Word, and are full of faith. In the Book of Acts it says that there was a need to appoint some over the business, and the criteria was to "seek out from among you seven men of good reputation, full of the Holy Spirit and wisdom, whom we might appoint" (Acts 6:3). This is another important reason why every local church and pastor needs a master craftsman to help them put the living stones together, so that the house of God is built correctly, and lives are built according to the pattern of the blueprint.

Would you like to know if this kind of generosity lives in you? The next time you have an opportunity to sow into the work of God, instead of deciding you're giving according to your needs, make a decision based on His thinking and heart, remembering His desire to be lavish and abundant, *then* give what you think is right. Make this a habit whenever you have an opportunity to give, always being mindful of love and generosity as your motive. After some time, your mindset will be transformed. God has already placed this desire in your heart, and you really want to give generously, so go ahead and live a little more in His abundant grace. As you practice this kind of giving, it will put to death any remaining spirit or mindset of poverty that was working to steal from you. Believing in God's love for you, and giving generously is truly the way that you honor God.

ALL ABOUT HONOR

God is our Father, the One who has created all things and given to all things life. Everything we have, and everything we are is because of Him. A son honors his father, and a servant his master. "If then I am the Father, where is My honor? And if I am a Master, where is My reverence?" (Mal. 1:6).

Sadly, throughout the Bible, we see God's people failing to honor the Father and show Him respect. In spite of all He had done for them and the fact that He provided everything they could possibly need in abundance, He still had to reprimand them for dreadful behavior. They chose not to reverence, respect, and honor God. Instead, they brought Him the second best, "But cursed be the deceiver who has in his flock a male, and takes a vow, but sacrifices to the Lord what is blemished" (Mal. 1:14).

I know you may be thinking, *Yes but that's Old Testament, and we live in the New!* Although that is true, it's also true that the Old points to the New; it is a marker for the New. As a chosen and special people who are inhabited by the Spirit of the living God, drinking of His Spirit and His Word, we should not only be fulfilling the Old, but living in the abundance and grace of the New. What they did in the Old is nothing to what we should be living in as New creations.

He is our Father through Christ—He is our Creator, the King of the universe. If everything we have and are comes from Him, surely we should be giving back to Him great honor. Honor is the substance of glory; so as we honor him rightly, we will see His glory. The idea of honoring also applies to ministers in the church.

WORTHY OF HONOR

Concerning the church, we should not think of caring for ministers as "payment," but rather as a way of honoring them. The ministry is worthy of honor. When speaking to Timothy, Paul says, "Let the elders who rule well be counted worthy of double honor, especially those who labor in the word and doctrine" (1 Tim. 5:17). Paul makes it clear that he is not referring to honor that is only spoken when he says, "For the Scripture says, 'You shall not muzzle an ox while it treads out the grain,' and, 'The laborer is worthy of his wages'" (1 Tim. 5:18). Quite clearly Paul is talking about wages and the fact that honor is shown in material blessing.

The apostle Paul was a hardworking sacrificial minister. He knew what it meant to work in the secular field as well as in ministry. To do the works of God and fulfill the commission upon his life, he often had to do both at the same time. He did it because he had to do it, but that didn't necessarily make it right, and although he learned from the Lord through having to do it, neither did that make it right. The right way was that the Church should have honored him by looking after him and making sure that he, like Jesus, had everything he needed in order to live and fulfill his ministry commission.

At times you can hear Paul's frustration "...is it only Barnabas and I who have no right to refrain from working?" (1 Cor. 9:6). Here was the totally committed and devoted apostle Paul with an incredible commission from the Lord, laying the foundation of Christ in the lives of believers everywhere, building the Church and unfolding the blueprint for their lives, and yet working to meet his own needs because the Church—the people who were receiving the rich Word that God had imparted to him—were not looking after their own!

Sadly, this legacy has continued in the Church. Many have even defended this practice as "spiritual," but there is nothing spiritual about lack or poverty. It has nothing to do with God. It has everything to do with selfishness, greed, and the way unredeemed people live, which the enemy hooks into and uses to his own ends.

Remember:

- ❖ You are born again by His Spirit.

- ❖ Your life is new; you have new love within you.

- ❖ Your new love is the love of God.

❖ Be selfless, not selfish.

❖ Live to give.

Paul makes an impassioned plea to those who will listen and obey, "Whoever goes to war at his own expense? Who plants a vineyard and does not eat of its fruit? Or who tends a flock and does not drink of the milk of the flock?" (1 Cor. 9:7). I think what Paul is trying to say, as diplomatically as possible is, "If I have raised up disciples and sons, if I have unfolded a whole new plan, a blueprint for your lives, if I have planted churches and taught, if I have equipped and trained, if I have given of myself tirelessly and without thought of myself for your benefit, should I not partake of all that I have sown?"

> *Do I say these things as a mere man? Or does not the law say the same also? For it is written in the law of Moses, "You shall not muzzle an ox while it treads out the grain." Is it the oxen God is concerned about? Or does He say it altogether for our sakes? For our sakes, no doubt, this is written, that he who plows should plow in hope, and he who threshes in hope should be partaker of his hope. If we have sown spiritual things for you, is it a great thing if we reap your material things?* (1 Corinthians 9:8-11)

I find it incredibly sad that Paul even had to say these things. Very little has changed since those days. It seems that finance is the most talked about of all subjects, both within and outside church. Yet those who have given so much and sacrificially laid down their lives to bring the church to maturity still find themselves having to uphold their own cause.

RESTORATION AND REFORMATION

In these days, many churches don't have an apostolic ministry; therefore, they do not understand apostolic life, or live in the revelation and grace of it. They do not enter into this blueprint for life, and therefore are unable to experience the fullness of this life that Christ has for each one of us.

Even many new churches, including those that are evangelic and Charismatic who perhaps even have had an initial understanding of these things, do not seem to have taken these words to heart. But in the days to come, I believe there will be both a restoration and a reformation, which brings forth a truly apostolic people—people living in a pattern of life designed by the Master Craftsman.

Sacrificial giving is part of the normal, everyday apostolic Christian life. It means giving from a heart filled with love that is always desiring and thinking of ways to build and bless another. It's giving from a place of faith. Without faith, it's not only impossible to please God, but it can also result in great stress, even to the point of a nervous breakdown when we attempt to live a real Christian life in any other way. The apostolic life of faith takes us on a journey that passes stations such as *not enough, through nearly enough, past just enough, and into more than enough.* It sees who God is, what He has, is assured by the truth, and then embraces and confesses it with great strength. It builds something in Heaven that is then seen manifest on the earth.

Our Heart's Desire

Apostolic finance can only be administered by those who are also on this journey themselves, and who desire to be completely free from a mindset of poverty, those who are being transformed and conformed into His image. This means men and women who are generous on every occasion.

Apostolic finance is administered from a heart desiring to *honor* rather than *pay*. It comes through those who give willingly and zealously, not those who give grudgingly, of necessity, or sparingly. It can be ordered and given with instruction, as "on the first day of the week," prepared giving as "I am sending a brother ahead to receive the offering…" and should involve everyone.

Apostolic ministry will always exhort the people of God to do all these things, not forgetting to teach about tithing, which is an *initial* response to the goodness of God and honors Him as our Father. This will not be taught in terms of the law, but rather impart heart revelation so that every member of the Body of Christ might live rightly, and be blessed in their giving. Sacrificial giving should become your normal, everyday lifestyle.

> **The blueprint of life includes journeys through not enough, nearly enough, just enough, into more than enough.**

Neither is apostolic teaching without concern for the poor and needy who we are instructed to bless (see Gal. 2:10; Acts 11:29-30; 2 Cor. 8:1-6). Nor will it overlook the widows and orphans, making sure that they are widows indeed (see 1 Tim. 5:1-13). It will also address sowing into the mission field, being watchful where and how, knowing that the field into which it sows is bringing forth good fruit. And, of course, the teaching will address the care we should have for each other in the Body of believers.

No Needy Among Them

Now all who believed were together, and had all things in common, and sold their possessions and goods, and divided them among all, as anyone had need (Acts 2:44-45).

Although this passage from Acts 2 may sound like a "New Age commune" where everything goes and everybody does as they please, it really wasn't like that at all. In the early church there was unity with diversity, a strong sense of purpose, and oneness of heart and mind. There was also discipleship training and equipping constantly taking place, coupled with a real sense of social awareness and a strong leadership team.

The fruit of this apostolic lifestyle was amazing in that there were no needy people among them. They loved and cared for each other. They shared what they had and experienced no lack. There were certain things that they automatically did as an accepted part of normal Christian living—which we would refer to as disciplines—and as they did these things they saw results. We read in Acts 4, "Nor was there anyone among them who lacked, for all who were possessors of lands and houses sold them, and brought the proceeds of the things that they sold, and laid them at the apostles' feet; and they distributed to each as anyone had need" (Acts 4:34-35).

Beyond Tithes and Offerings

We can see that all need was erased and there was no lack of any kind. They weren't just tithing and bringing the usual offerings, nor were they merely supplying saints in other regions; they were doing all these things plus selling their possessions and goods to take care of brethren who were with them every day. This caused a flow of finance to pour into the house of God; notice also that the believers who sold their houses and lands brought the proceeds voluntarily. They were not told or commanded to do this, they desired to do it.

We should also observe that when they brought the proceeds, it was "laid at the apostles' feet." This demonstrates a number of very important and wonderful things. First of all, it demonstrates that the believers *trusted* their leaders. The believers did not demand or tell the leaders where they should put the proceeds. No, once they had chosen to sell their lands and houses, they took the next radical step of giving that money as to the Lord. *They sowed it into the Kingdom without any demands or expectations.*

A CORPORATE VISION

It also demonstrates that they understood a "corporate vision." They believed in something and Someone more than themselves. They had a purpose and a vision *together* for the King and His Kingdom. Life was no longer just about themselves or their own family. It was not about their prosperity or success, as much as it was about His Kingdom coming on the earth. Not only this, but they also understood something of the sovereign call and appointing that God in His wisdom puts within a man or woman of God who has been made a "gift" ministry. As it says in Ephesians 4, "And He Himself gave some to be apostles, prophets, pastors, evangelists and teachers" (Eph. 4:11). Not only did the disciples receive the apostles, but they also released them to be and do what God had called and commissioned them to do.

As called and chosen apostles (master craftsmen), they had wisdom, grace, and an anointing to see and build in a way that caused the Church to be built up and glorify the King. So when the believers "laid the proceeds at the apostles' feet," they understood that the apostles had the grace and the wisdom to know how and what to do with what was put before them!

It was the apostles who "distributed to each as anyone had need." They were the ones who oversaw the ministries looking after the flock, who were in prayer and received insight and guidance from the Spirit of God and regular reports from the ministries, thus having the wisdom to lead His people into all that He had for them.

His Kingdom Come

I am sure that in these days there are those who desire to give. They want to see the Kingdom come and God's will done. However, there are many who want to do it *their* way as opposed to His way. Many still have a need to show others that *they* are the ones who have supplied the gift. Not only do they expose their pride, but they also expose their independence and lack of understanding in the fact that the church is to cooperate corporately. Clearly they have not fully been able to trust those whom the Lord has set over them to care for them, nor are the leaders able to trust them. Sadly, they not only end up undermining themselves, but in the end, they actually steal the glory of God for themselves.

Glorifying God

The main reason that the Lord wants finances to come into the house is that when money is sown into the lives of others and needs are met, no one but the Lord gets the glory!

Remember what was discussed at the beginning of this chapter, the way finances are handled exposes the motives of the heart. Christians all over the world want to see the glory of God; they want to experience the presence of God, and are praying continually for revival and restoration. The only way this can begin to happen is when the *least* of all—money—is handled rightly from godly motives in the hearts of His people.

God is very serious about finance, and He also knows and sees clearly the motives of our hearts toward money:

> But a certain man named Ananias, with Sapphira his wife, sold a possession. And he kept back part of the proceeds, his wife also being aware of it, and brought a certain part and laid it at the apostles' feet. But Peter said, "Ananias, why has Satan filled your heart to lie to the Holy Spirit and keep back part of the price of the land for yourself? While it remained was it not your own? And after you sold it, was it not in your own control? Why have you conceived this thing in your heart? You have not lied to men

but to God." Then Ananias, hearing these words, fell down and breathed his last... (Acts 5:1-5).

There was something in the heart of Ananias and his wife that wanted the glory. They were stealing glory from God, because they wanted to be seen as laying everything before the Lord as the other believers had done. However, they were deceiving themselves and those around them; they were lying. I believe they could have been honest by giving just part of the proceeds and saying so, that would have been fine. In the end, God is very serious about your heart.

How you use the resources that He has given you exposes your motives—that is what God is paying attention to, the motives of your heart. When you are totally His, then the thing that drives you will be the same thing that moved Him to send Christ—love—and it will show in the way you handle finances.

This is apostolic life in the sphere of finance. It may not be where you are yet, but it certainly is where you are going.

Your blueprint of life from Jesus means that:

❖ Your blueprint is part of a greater blueprint that involves many others.

❖ You are not primarily concerned with yourself.

❖ You are concerned with God and His family.

❖ Your heart is filled with His love.

❖ You understand that it is more blessed to give than to receive.

❖ You love to give all that you have to Him who gave His all and all that He has.

Chapter Thirteen

SHAME AND REPROACH

Who wants a blueprint for life that would include shame and reproach? Not me for one, and I am certain neither do you.

What we need to acknowledge and understand is that the Lord of Life, Jesus Himself, the great Master Craftsman, the great Apostle, the One who not only brought to us this blueprint and pattern for living life, but is our example about how to live in it and bring forth life in every situation and circumstance. He is the One to whom we should look and set our eyes upon. He endured, we also must endure.

> *looking unto Jesus, the Author and Finisher of our faith, who for the joy set before Him endured the cross, despising the shame, and has sat down at the right hand of the throne of God* (Hebrews 12:2).

IS IT WORTH IT?

Recently, I was praying through some difficult and challenging issues resulting from things that I have personally had to navigate through during my life of ministry. They also applied to situations and issues that others were facing; things for which I was trying to help them find grace and mercy in their time of need. I was affected in a deep way by these various situations and concerns.

I again found myself asking the Lord if it was all really worth it. I do not confess this lightly, and it is not something that I have done often. However, there have been times when I have found things nearly too much to carry, when circumstances and emotions make the journey seem too overwhelming to continue. Such seasons are accompanied by an incredible sense of loneliness, (despite the fact that I am surrounded by kind and loving family), that sometimes seemed to be more than I could endure.

In recent years, these seasons have become more intense. As I have considered this, and without being proud or arrogant, I realized that I was carrying something of the burden for the Body of Christ that the Great Apostle experienced. Please understand that I am *not* saying everything that afflicts me, every pain or difficulty that I experience, is for others. What I am saying is that in some way and at some times on my journey, I have indeed had to carry the afflictions of Christ for the sake of His Body, as have the churches that I've established by the grace of God.

In saying these things some may think that I sound proud and believe I have gone too far—that I am being "super spiritual" or am living in falsehood. I ask that you hold your judgment because throughout this chapter I clarify how I feel and explain my heart, in hopes of helping those who may feel similar burdens.

The Scriptures leave no doubt that any genuine and authentic apostolic life and ministry carries with it some suffering, persecution, and reproach. The suffering of which I speak is not in ill health. The Word of the Lord is clear; we have been healed by His stripes. The suffering I am referring to has to do with the "weight and burden" of the churches, and the realization of the desire that this building ministry, the apostolic ministry, carries to see the Body of Christ walking in maturity. The persecution is sometimes external, although there can also be a spiritual, satanic persecution toward apostolic ministry. Paul speaks of this in his own life as being due to the nature of apostolic revelation. The apostle Paul says:

> ...*in weariness and toil, in sleeplessness often, in hunger and thirst, in fastings often, in cold and nakedness—besides the other things, what comes upon me daily: my deep concern* [burden] *for all the churches. Who is weak, and I am not weak? Who is made to stumble and I do not burn with indignation? If I must boast, I will boast in the things which concern my infirmity* (2 Corinthians 11:27-30).

Paul clearly carries a deep concern for the Church. The weaknesses of others affect him; the trials of others concern him; and these things affect not only his overall sense of well-being, but he also often felt the burden of concern in his physical body.

The Scripture leaves no doubt that any genuine apostolic ministry carries with it some suffering, reproach, and persecution. Satanic persecution can come because of apostolic revelation. This revelation is building and transforming the Body of Christ and bringing it into maturity and fullness.

> **The Scripture leaves no doubt that any genuine apostolic ministry carries with it some suffering, reproach, and persecution.**

Later, in the following chapter of Second Corinthians, Paul continues to talk about his apostolic ministry to the churches:

> *And lest I should be exalted above measure by the abundance of the revelations, a thorn in the flesh was given to me, a messenger of Satan to buffet me, lest I be exalted above measure. Concerning this thing I pleaded with the Lord three times that it might depart from me. And He said to me, My grace is sufficient for you, for My strength is made perfect in weakness. Therefore most gladly I will rather boast in my infirmities, that the power of Christ may rest upon me (2 Corinthians 12:7-9).*

APOSTOLIC LIFE AND MINISTRY

We are talking about apostolic life and ministry. In the passage from Second Corinthians 12:7-9, Paul links his sharing in the burden for all the churches to his boasting about his infirmity. As we read through chapters 11 and 12, we begin to see the often daunting consequences of living an apostolic life.

Many ministers today, especially in the Western church, proclaim that such *suffering* for the sake of the Body is no longer valid. They maintain that it was because of the nature of Paul's revelations that this "messenger" was given.

The nature of any genuine apostolic ministry brings life to the Word of God. It brings the Word to life in those who receive it, adding deep meaning and bringing life-changing transformation and building through revelation and insight gathered in His presence. Of course, when ministry begins to move in the "mystery" of the revelation from the deep places of God's heart, then it is a major threat to the enemies of God. And though they have been completely and utterly disarmed by the work of Christ's death and resurrection, that victory is administered and becomes manifest as the Church is obedient to and walks in its fullness. This cannot happen without authentic apostolic ministry making it known fully and continually in the earth.

Paul had insight and revelation as an apostolic minister. He also *carried* the weight and burden of all the specific churches and the Body of Christ in general. He desired to see it come into fullness and maturity to the point that it made his bones ache. He wept; he experienced sleepless nights; he toiled and gave himself tirelessly to this end. When he saw his desire being fulfilled, it made his heart leap for joy; when it was not fulfilled, his heart missed a beat in despair.

For some reason, something attached itself to Paul, finding a place in him that could be used at different times to cause him great pain and hardship. Many have discussed what this could have been. Some say a physical illness; others say it was the persecution that followed him everywhere he went.

However, I think that it is clear from the text. Paul says it was a "thorn in his flesh." It seems obvious to me that this was something that affected his physical being, his flesh; at the same time he makes no bones about calling this "a messenger from Satan" (see 2 Cor. 12:7).

Could it then be that the burden he carried in his heart and spirit for the Church, and the revelation which he had been shown, had such a deep impact upon him that it had opened his natural, physical being up in such a way that a messenger of satan could prick him? As the enemy attacked him with a thorn, which expressed itself as a physical condition, it caused him to continually humble himself before the Lord. Could this sense of weakness or infirmity have left him feeling that his only recourse was to call on God? Although this evil, satanic being intended to cause Paul's downfall with this affliction, it actually served to propel him even further into the mystery of God, discovering His plan and purpose, which Paul then revealed to the Church.

Suffering and Maturity

In his letter to the Colossians, Paul says some very interesting things. He begins the Book by once again declaring "Paul, an apostle of Jesus Christ by the will of God...." He goes on to state clearly all that Christ has accomplished, right through to verse 24 where he says:

> *I now rejoice in my sufferings for you, and fill up in my flesh what is lacking in the afflictions of Christ, for the sake of His body, which is the church, of which I became a minister according to the stewardship from God which was given to me for you, to fulfill the word of God, the mystery which has been hidden from ages and from generations, but now has been revealed to His saints* (Colossians 1:24-26).

From what Paul is saying, it seems that the things he had to endure in his apostolic ministry were not for his own sake; rather they have something to do with the maturing of the Body of Christ. Now, in the natural, there is much that I do not care for about what I am saying! The personal ramifications are not a pleasant thought. Although it is not something that I have heard others speak of in regard to the apostolic life and ministry, biblically it certainly seems to be a significant part of it.

I am, however, absolutely certain that there is a suffering experienced in which we are partaking of the sufferings of Christ, and I do not believe that it is just in terms of persecution.

Those who are ministers of His apostolic building grace to the church, those who are administering the blueprint of life, may experience satanic persecution, reproach, and shame. This will cause them to know His grace in greater depth. It will also propel them further into the mystery of God so that they can administer this blueprint of life in greater grace and power, resulting in the Body coming into fullness and maturity.

SIMON OF CYRENE

One morning as I was speaking to the Lord about some of the sufferings that I have endured over the years, I felt strongly that He spoke to me about Simon of Cyrene. This Bible character is not a man I had studied earlier, or of whom I had ever thought much about.

In the Gospel of Mark 15:21 it says, "Then they compelled a certain man, Simon a Cyrenian, the father of Alexandra and Rufus, as he was coming out of the country and passing by, to bear His Cross." Here was a man "compelled" to carry the cross of Jesus. He had no choice in the matter; he didn't want to do it; he didn't choose to do it; but he had no choice. This was not his cross to bear—it was the cross of Jesus.

At the time, Simon did not realize what he was doing. It was not just that he helped Jesus bear His cross—the cross is symbolic of the weight of sin, the burden of grief and pain, and the desperation and deep sorrow of man—he was actually sharing the weight and burden of what Jesus was carrying for you and me.

Jesus said that no one could follow Him and be His disciple without carrying his own cross. Each of us have our own, or have had our own, natural desires and wants—our own selfish thought life and carnal desires that need to be put to death. That's our cross. Putting these things to death is often a daily exercise.

> **Selfish thought life and carnal desires need to be put to death.**

But this was the cross of Jesus, and it *has been* carried. *Our sin and transgression, our pain and grief have all been carried by Jesus; He has dealt with it all.* Having said that, isn't it possible that just as Simon was compelled to carry Jesus' cross, there are also those who share in His ministry, who are moved by His heart of compassion and allowed to share in the afflictions of Christ for the sake of His Body?

LOOKING FROM AFAR

It's incredible to think that Jesus' family, friends, disciples, and hundreds of others watched Him go through this completely alone. No one chose to help Him; no one chose to carry His cross for Him. Most of the people who surrounded Jesus on His way to die for their sins were spitting at Him, accusing Him, mocking and despising Him, and yet *He did it for all of them.* Even those who loved him "looked on from afar."

I believe that there was a point at which Jesus could no longer bear the pain alone. If He had continued to carry His burden without help, it would have caused even greater physical pain and disfigured him, perhaps his flesh falling away—so for a short while, another was called upon to share His suffering, and to bear His cross.

As Simon walked with the cross, he walked out of the city of Jerusalem—the city that did not want to bear the reproach of the cross of Jesus; the people who did not want to bear the shame and reproach of the cross of Jesus. They wanted it outside the city. They didn't want to be tainted with this Man's blood.

Jesus was the great Apostle. He came to bring a whole New Covenant, an incredible message declaring the love of the Father, the reality of God's Kingdom, and the promises of God that were now available to all. He came to bring something *wonderful,* something *new* and *delightful.* He carried with Him a pattern by which we can live and have fullness of life, but in order to bring in the new, He had to first fulfill the old.

Outside the Camp

Simon was compelled to carry the cross of Jesus. He had no choice. With this burden, he also had to carry shame, reproach, and suffering. He shared in the taunts, the mocking, and the hatred. He didn't want any of it—but he had no choice. In the Gospel of Matthew 27:32 it says, "Now as they came out...." Simon and Jesus had to come out of the city, bearing the shame and reproach as they carried the cross.

> *Therefore Jesus also, that He might sanctify the people with His own blood, suffered **outside the gate,** Therefore let us go forth to Him, **outside the camp,** bearing His reproach* (Hebrews 13:12-13).

It was only when Jesus was outside the gate, outside the camp, that He could fulfill the old and bring in the new.

I am certain that all genuine apostolic ministries are called to share in the sufferings of Christ. They have part in *bearing the reproach* of the cross. Perhaps, as with Simon, there is no choice in the matter. They are compelled to take part in bearing the reproach. Simon carried the cross to ease the pain on the body of Christ. Simon would never know the depth of suffering or pain that Christ experienced, but in some small way he would share in His sufferings. He would know some measure of the great cost of seeing the Kingdom of God come on earth.

Master builders, apostolic ministries, those who desire to build within the Kingdom through the incredible selfless love of the Lord and by His Spirit and the love that He brings to us, are sometimes required to endure reproach, shame, and persecution so that the Church comes into the fullness of His divine purpose.

Apostolic life and ministry suffers, "that I may know Him and the power of His resurrection, and the fellowship of His sufferings, being conformed to His death, if, by any means, I may attain to the resurrection from the dead" (Phil. 3:10-11).

They, in part, carry reproach and shame, not for any reason linked to salvation, because that was all completed upon the cross by Jesus, but that the Body of Christ might come to fullness and maturity.

Apostolic life desires to bring the new; it desires to unfold the blueprint of life and bring forth the fullness of that life—new spheres, new dimensions, new assignments, and most of all, the New Covenant in resurrection power to the earth. A vital part of seeing these things accomplished includes bearing shame and reproach *outside* the camp, and also experiencing suffering in terms of the weight and burden of the churches.

Being outside the camp often entails loneliness. It sometimes involves being misunderstood, misinterpreted, and discredited. The door can feel as though it's closing and you are being locked out. It seems that the very people to whom the promises of God belong, are the ones who expel and exclude the ones who can bring those promises and help make them become reality within individual lives and also the corporate life of the church. Any people looking to see lives built correctly and properly, any genuine apostolic people will realize the truth of this to some extent. If they have hearts to bless, a desire to build, and want to see the Kingdom come to earth with the fullness of His life and power, then they will be misunderstood, misaligned, mocked, and laughed at. They will be the target of accusations and lies and experience persecution of some type.

Apostolic leaders will realize and experience this cross even more, *and will do so in ever-increasing measure, as they break through into new dimensions of Kingdom power and authority.*

What Is Not Being Said

I am *not* saying that we are to be sick and suffering. I am not believing or standing in faith for that. I believe absolutely that Jesus died not only for our sins and transgressions, but also for our sicknesses, pains, and infirmities. He carried all that ails humankind to the cross and dealt with it there—there He destroyed the devil and disarmed all principalities and powers.

What I have outlined is the apostolic life—the life of Jesus in and through apostolic ministry—that in some way carries a burden and a weight of responsibility for the Body of Christ, as well as feeling and living some of the shame and reproach that Jesus carried. In order to fulfill His purpose of reconciling humanity back to God, restoring us and bringing us into the fullness of God's purpose and plan, this cannot be avoided. I do not fully understand, or like, this principle, and yet it is clear from writings about Jesus' and Paul's suffering, that shame and reproach are part of the apostolic call placed in their hearts by the Father.

As these things are true and an integral part of the apostolic tapestry, we will not deny them.

Chapter Fourteen

WALKING IN THE BLUEPRINT

Throughout this book I have used interchangeable words—pattern-blueprint, master craftsman-apostle—as these words describe more or less the same kind of thing.

With everything that God does, He creates and builds perfectly. He has a plan, a designed pattern; He does not just hope for a good future, nor is He just waiting to see how something might turn out. He knows. He sees it and has a blueprint that lays it out perfectly. He builds foundationally, which means that everything pertaining to life is found and established in Christ. It is built of that foundation. There is nothing that can be or will be that is not in Him and from Him.

Of course there are many people on planet Earth doing many things, busy and working. However, Jesus made it clear that outside of Him nothing can be done that will have real lasting value, "Without Me you can do nothing" (John 15:5). This is a principle that we have a tendency to forget. Our life upon the earth goes by very quickly. This is not it, there is so much more, everything that Jesus said was coming from His Father's heart and was in the light of eternity is waiting for you to experience.

Since He is building into eternity, everything that He is building is following a designed pattern, a specific purpose that He has determined. He is not rushing. He is not in a hurry to lay foundations and do a mega build that in the end brings forth only partial blessing. He wants it established, firm, strong, grounded, so that He can keep building into it and upon it, causing reproduction of life and fruitfulness.

He is the Master Craftsman, the One who builds according to His own blueprint. So if we want to be like Him, we have to seek out this blueprint, this pattern of life that He has laid down and also lived for us as an example. He is the One who lived on the earth in the fullness of God's life. If we want a full and purposeful life, then we have to seek out the blueprint of life that He has made clear, and desire to follow after Him.

Becoming apostolic, then, is about having a hunger and desire to build solidly and soundly on the correct foundation; it is about finding the blueprint of life that Jesus designed for us so that we can have a life with the Father *now* that is abundant and full.

For many years there has been a renewing taking place within the church; in some parts of the world, the Spirit of God has been reminding and speaking to His people about the need for apostolic restoration and reformation.

> **The Word of the Lord declares that the church is to be a prophetic and apostolic people.**

The Word of the Lord has declared that the church is to be a prophetic people and an apostolic people. Much teaching has been given, and many books have been written on the subjects of apostles and prophets as well as the fivefold gift ministries. I believe that it is without doubt that the heart and purpose of God is for this very thing to happen, but few have experienced the reality of what is within these great truths. Why is this the case?

LIVING THE REALITY

It is one thing to proclaim a biblical truth, but quite another to live in the reality of that biblical truth.

There is a definite blueprint for life brought to us by Jesus Himself and exemplified by Him. This blueprint outlines and gives clear directives and instructions of how we can live and what that life will involve. He wants this for us. Yet to live in the reality of it is not an easy thing.

As Jesus Himself made clear, "Enter by the narrow gate; for wide is the gate and broad is the way that leads to destruction, and there are many who go in by it. Because narrow is the gate and difficult [confined] is the way which leads to **life**, and there are few who find it" (Matt 7:13-14).

Jesus is talking about finding *life*. The way to having and enjoying *life* is not easy. It would be absolutely impossible without the miracle of the new birth, a new spirit within us, and the Holy Spirit given to us, filling us with the very same love that He is and has.

Eventually, of course, we who are His children will all experience this overwhelming life. We sometimes think that as soon as we die we will enter into a blissful peaceful state and have nothing more to do. Wrong!

We will of course enter into His Kingdom where He, the King, has domain and where everyone and everything is given completely and utterly over to Him. But will we still learn? Of course. Will we have to go through change and keep developing? Of course. Will it be wonderful and glorious? Without any doubt!

But now, today in this day of salvation and the day of God's grace, right now by His Spirit and through His Word we are being built, shaped, transformed, and trained for the time to come. Even with His Spirit working with us and in us, it is not always easy. We have choices to make; we can choose what we want to do each and every day.

SELFISHNESS

The very core of apostolic Christianity is the giving of oneself to another in sacrificial love, and that speaks immediately to the biggest and gravest danger that the church faces—selfishness.

It is becoming clear that it is quite possible to be saved by the precious work of the Savior and at the same time continue to live life for yourself. In other words, many accept that Christ has died for their sin and that He rose from the dead, but they reject entirely that there is a need to follow in His footsteps and be transformed to be more like Him. Scripture declares:

If anyone desires to come after Me, let him deny himself, and take up his cross, and follow Me (Matthew 16:24).

For whom He foreknew, He also predestined to be conformed to the image of His Son... (Romans 8:29).

This is God's bottom line regarding everything that we anytime, anywhere are doing—to be made into His image.

IMAGE CONSULTANTS

Today we have image consultants, specialists who help people showcase themselves in the best light. They help people feel better about themselves, look their best, and present their strengths and abilities. This type of help is not necessarily wrong, but it is wholly wrong if we have not yet found out who we are and who we are not! There is much that we as Christians have to identify, confess, and face head-on before we can receive the promises of God that allow us to rule and reign as ambassadors and kings before our God.

> **Jesus' desire is to restore to us our true identity and build us internally into the person He always intended us to become.**

On Jesus finding us in His grace and saving us from our sin, His desire is also to restore to us our true identity and build us internally into the person He always intended us to become. To this person He can add dynamite power—*dunamis*–the same power that fell upon all those mentioned in the second chapter of Acts. This is exactly what He did and what happened with His disciples, "Now when Jesus looked at him, He said 'You are Simon the son of Jonah. You shall be called Cephas (which is translated, A Stone)" (John 1:42).

On meeting Simon the son of Jonah, Jesus declared a new name for him, Cephas. In doing this, He signaled that now that Simon was following Him, a new identity would be formed and shaped. The original DNA had been spoilt. Nonetheless, Simon was made unique, special, and very precious. Jesus would, through the anointed Word, deal with that which was spoiling and bring to life and add new values and virtues into Cephas' very being. He had been a fisherman, but this journey would give him all he needed to become an apostle.

The Master Builder Himself will build everyone who follows Him into the person they truly can become, and release them into new dimensions of life and love.

THE NEW PSEUDO CHRISTIAN

There is a generation of Christians who want the promises, the power, and the inheritance, but do not want to deny themselves—sometimes not even face themselves—thus hearing and desiring the promises, but then building themselves on top of self. They become what I term a "pseudo new Christian," saying the right things, looking outwardly prosperous and successful, but internally having never dealt (by the Spirit) with the old selfish self who wants everything he or she can get without having put into practice Kingdom principle number one—life comes from death. All life in the Kingdom is established on this one thing.

The Kingdom of God is not a *selfish* Kingdom but a *selfless* Kingdom. The only way that the Father could show us who He is every nanosecond of every minute of every day was to send Jesus His only begotten Son, His express image and the glory of His radiance (see Heb. 1:1-3) to the earth to give Himself completely and utterly for us.

Although this was a once for all action on the earth, it was a demonstration of how the Father, the Son, and the Holy Spirit, the godhead, actually love us all the time! This cross love, this sacrificial giving all the time love, is the love that God is. That is what the Kingdom of God is established in.

Therefore all selfishness has to be dealt with before we can enter into all that is prepared. Of course there will be those who are just saved, very new, and those who have just been born again, and we would not expect them to be able to enter into all that is prepared straight away.

But for those who have been Christians for many years, who have been following Christ and have been discipled in the Kingdom school, this is exactly what we would expect.

God cannot build His promises on the foundations of your old self. When Christ came and found you, He became the foundation upon which you were to build your life. That foundation must be laid internally by the Spirit and through the Word. The nature of the foundation changes from selfishness to selflessness. The Spirit of God does this within you as you become obedient.

Alas, sadly there will have been many who were "church goers" all their lives, who have sang the songs, read the stories, prayed some prayers, and even seen some blessing, but many of them on entering into the glory that is prepared may have to begin all over again!

THE PLUMB LINE

When I say that real Christianity is the giving up of oneself for another in sacrificial love, I realize that is a huge statement to make. It's an incredible plumb line with which we measure the heart, the motivations, and the activities of the church. I do not say it to sound biblically correct and good, I say it because I believe that this is the truth about what it means to be an apostolic church.

I use this plumb line upon myself and all that I do, the churches that I serve and lead, and the ministries I oversee. Of course I, too, fall short when I walk in my own natural ways and choose those things that are not right. Nonetheless, that does not alter the truth, nor should it cause any embarrassment.

THE SWINGING PENDULUM

Down the years, although the apostolic message has been reengaged and spoken about and brought as a fresh revelation, it has also—as all fresh insight and revelation to the people of God—been abused, misunderstood, and misaligned. When fresh revelation comes forth, the swing of the pendulum to find the right balance often overshoots into an extreme.

Have there been extremes? Of course. Has there been misuse? Have people been hurt? Sadly, we have to answer *yes* to these questions, as well as acknowledge that millions of Christians have not even given apostolic revelation any thought. Much teaching has been dispensational in nature.

This teaching asserts certain truths using only the Scriptures they want to use to uphold that particular truth, thus relegating all things apostolic to the time of Jesus walking on the earth or of the time to come.

Not only does Scripture make it absolutely clear that apostles and prophets are for today, but that they are significant and indispensable parts of God's plan for the restoration of both the church and all things. Church history also makes it clear that apostles and prophets have never disappeared. The sad fact that men did not want to receive and release them does not alter the truth and will not alter God's divine purpose.

Previously I outlined the way in which Jesus called to Himself twelve disciples who would become apostles. One of them became something else through his own choice, but the rest of them chose to become the men God intended. The Kingdom program for this process is called discipleship, the vehicle that not only transports us into the Kingdom to see it, receive it, and become it, but also teaches us how we can negotiate through the things of this world without crashing and in the end be worthy enough to be called one of His own.

THE SCHOOL OF DISCIPLESHIP

Discipleship includes servanthood, obedience, faithfulness, accountability, submission, trust, commitment, etc. Much of this comes to us as commands or directives from His Word. As we do the things we are commanded to do, we also become them so that the Word we hear becomes the Word we are—a letter of God's transforming power within us, "clearly you are an epistle of Christ, ministered by us, written not with ink but by the Spirit of the living God..." (2 Cor. 3:3). And at the same time showing God and ourselves that we do actually love Him, "He who does not love Me does not keep My words..." (John 14:24).

Loving Him takes us on a journey through discipleship into friendship and on into the real experience—not just the faith fact—of being sons and daughters as we enter into our inheritance in the right way for the Father and the Kingdom. We also begin to experience a measure of rule and reign, even upon the earth. This is when life on the earth becomes an exciting opportunity to do His will. To walk the blueprint of life this far is a considerable feat, and it may have been quite a difficult, but worthy, journey!

Many may have left and forsaken the way, some who began may no longer want to walk with or even know you. But to a true son, things become much clearer and more defined. Kingdom ways are opposed to the ways of this world, and instead of being overcome by worry and fear, by thoughts of what you cannot do and must not do, instead of living by rules and regulations, you find a life internally that has values and virtues that you know are His—and have become yours! *Now you want to overcome, rather than be overcome.*

SONS BECOME FATHERS

Every true son eventually becomes a father. But not every father is an apostle. From among the true sons who have become fathers, those who have been called and set apart as apostles can be received and released into the church. This is exactly the same for women. There is no difference in the process. By saying this I am not undermining headship or submission.

THE UPSIDE DOWN KINGDOM

Let this mind be in you which was also in Christ Jesus, who, being in the form of God, did not consider it robbery to be equal with God, but made Himself of no reputation, taking the form of a bondservant, and coming in the likeness of men, And being found in appearance as a man, He humbled Himself and became obedient to the point of death, even the death of the cross. Therefore God also has highly exalted Him and given Him the name which is above every name, that at the name of Jesus every knee should bow in heaven and of those on earth, and that every tongue should confess that Jesus Christ is Lord, to the glory of God the Father (Philippians 2:5-11).

With Jesus' humility and obedience came authority and exaltation. His exaltation came only as He gave His life "even the death of the Cross." Although He exercised more authority and released more power than anybody else on the face of the earth, yet it was still a small part of what He originally had and what He would receive following His death and resurrection.

If this was true of Jesus the only begotten Son of God, then it must also be true for us. Kingdom authority must find itself and come out of what we call humility and meekness. I have spoken of this previously, needless to say that real Kingdom authority, although invested within the ministry gift itself, finds a dwelling place when internally a believer of Christ is walking in obedience and humility.

Moses, the great leader of the people of Israel, found this to be true also; the Scripture says of him that he was the meekest person in the whole world. Perhaps that is why Moses exercised a truly incredible amount of authority and power.

THE FOUNDATION

The foundation of our faith is Christ Jesus, "For no other foundation can anyone lay than that which is laid, which is Jesus Christ" (1 Cor. 3:11). The cross shows the depth of His love toward us, demonstrates His love in action toward us, and how He loves us all the time.

As Jesus served us and gave Himself for us, the power of the Kingdom, which is established within His sacrificial love, was released upon the earth in ever-increasing measure. Because He always moves in this love and righteousness, the power and authority of the Kingdom was and is seen clearly all the time.

As the Son of God, Jesus was ruling and reigning through the empowering of the Holy Spirit. The Holy Spirit stayed within Him and upon Him because He was continually of a humble heart, continually obedient to the Father and His attitude was always that of laying down His life in order to have and receive the life of the Spirit within the Kingdom.

When Jesus called His disciples to Himself, He effectively set them on this same course. Their journey would be like His. This was His blueprint; they, and we, would follow in His footsteps.

The prophets before them, in the Old Testament, often had to walk a very costly journey in order to bring the Kingdom to the earth. Many were persecuted and often died for the sake of the Kingdom. The twelve would be no different. Just like the great Apostle Himself, they too would lay down their lives to bring forth the life of the Kingdom. Even if they had not had to die physically for the sake of the Kingdom, all of them died to themselves to live for Him and help establish His Kingdom on the earth.

Remember:

❖ The foundation of your life is Christ.

❖ This foundation has to be established within you.

❖ You are a new creation, born again by the Spirit of God.

❖ His love is within you.

❖ The selfless love of God is poured out within you.

❖ You are becoming selfless.

RECOGNIZING THE COST

Any minister, ministry, or church that wants to be apostolic must understand and recognize the real cost in becoming apostolic. When God in His sovereign wisdom called forth and set apart these gifts and gave them for His Church, He put within them the ability and willingness to give themselves completely first to the Lord and then for the Church. They would not just teach about Kingdom, but as they gave themselves for the Kingdom, they would also be able to understand apostolic revelation and mystery and unfold it in such a way that the Church could receive it and become it themselves.

UNIQUE ANOINTING AND WISDOM

Apostles have a very unique anointing that helps them lay the foundation and build with wisdom, centering all of their building "in Him."

According to the grace of God which was given to me, as a wise master builder I have laid the foundation, and another builds on it. But let each one take heed how he builds on it. For no other foundation can anyone lay than that which is laid, which is Jesus Christ (1 Corinthians 3:10-11).

A pastor, evangelist, teacher, and prophet are also incredibly needful to the building up of the Body and they, too, have a specific anointing to do what they been called to do. However, a pastor or a teacher does not have the anointing or the wisdom to lay a foundation in the same way that an apostle does. The pastor may know the pattern, he may know how the building should look, but what he does not have is the necessary anointing and wisdom to actually set apart, release, and set in place the living stones that together are being built into a spiritual temple.

The pastor and other gift ministries have a very important and crucial part in the foundational building, both within the individual believer and corporately, under the oversight and with the wisdom that comes through the apostolic gift they together can build the building. Apostles "see" foundationally; they know instinctively what is needed and how and when it should be released. They know the criteria for the job and are able to impart and give powerful release to those appointed toward that function (see Acts 6:1-7).

Those who are building gifts, specifically apostles, have a very unique anointing and wisdom within them. They see with foundational understanding. No matter what the issue of challenge may be when they look at it, they see it from the foundation upward. The foundation, or lack of it, is where they zoom in. Their unique gift allows them to build or rebuild someone from this place.

Many local churches suffer greatly because they do not have the right gifts in the right place; this of course impedes growth and hinders the purposes of God within that local assembly. The pastor may well see what the building should look like and desire it to be according to the pattern, but sadly they do not have the anointing or wisdom to make it happen.

EXTENSIONS AND EXPRESSIONS OF CHRIST

All the characteristics of Christ as the great Apostle can be received by those He has sovereignly called and appointed to be an apostolic gift ministry into the church. They are, in fact, an extension and expression of who He is within the church.

Apostles are appointed by Christ Himself not by man. They are gifts to the church and as such must be received and treated with respect and honor. Although they are not appointed by man, they are recognized as ministers by the church but more particularly by leaders and ministries within the church. Although apostles can be appointed only by Christ Himself, they have the authority of Christ to appoint and release other ministries and elders within the church.

These extensions and expressions of Christ Himself are to be received and released into the church. Not just things taught, but life that is caught. *Eventually, individual believers within the body become more and more apostolic in their thinking and being*—this in turn effecting the whole body of believers who themselves together are becoming more and more as the great Apostle, laying down their lives for another in sacrificial love.

That truly is what an apostolic church should look like. Builders with the same DNA of Christ think like this, talk like this, and walk in the same manner.

Apostles, master craftsmen, are gifts from God—building gifts. They have specific tools to build. Apostles have wisdom and anointing to set things in order. As they are received and released within the church, the whole church takes on these same characteristics and nature, thus becoming apostolic—selfless builders giving their lives and love for others.

Chapter Fifteen

YOUR CHOICE

The revelation and truth of what has been laid out within the pages of this book are found also within the covers of your Bible. There is nothing that I have written that has not already been said. Even though I am teaching through these pages and you are reading these words, it is in fact the Holy Spirit Himself who teaches you.

> *But you have an anointing from the Holy One, and you know all things. I have not written to you because you do not know the truth, but because you know it, and that no lie is of the truth* (1 John 2:20-21).

You know the truth. The reason you know the truth is because the Holy One is within you and He has anointed you with His own understanding and ability to see. You may well have felt an "amen" deep down on the inside as you have read some of what is written. This is because He lives in You. He is teaching you. Because you know the truth, you also know when it is not the truth but a lie!

Despite the fact that you may well sense an "amen" deep down does not automatically mean that you will immediately begin to *do* the truth. Often this is where your dilemma lies. You hear the truth and say "amen" to that truth because you recognize that it is truth. However, for the truth that you have heard to become *your truth*, you have to submit to it yourself.

In other words you have got to make it your own truth. It's already the truth that belongs to the Holy Spirit, the Father, and the Son. Therefore they agree with it.

Sometimes although we know it is the truth, we don't always want to *do* it because it inevitably has a certain cost. This is when we have to deny ourselves and allow the truth to take its place within our whole being. Our thinking has to be transformed. We need to *choose* to submit to and obey the truth. We need to say *yes* to what God has already said *yes* to. How much we want to change and be transformed is entirely within our own will. We must *choose* to obey.

YOUR FREE CHOICE

God (and by using this term I refer to the Three in One; God the Father, God the Son, and God the Holy Spirit) will never violate your free will. He has given every one of us free choice. Therefore, although He desires to do things, and say things, moving and impacting your life in specific ways, the way of love, He will never violate the right He gave you to choose.

Obviously, this means that you can choose to do right or wrong. You can choose to use your mind, emotions, intellect, and your body in any way you desire. These choices may not be the way that God would do something, but nonetheless, you have the choice.

YOUR DECISIONS USUALLY INVOLVE OTHERS

Naturally, there are consequences that come with the choices you make. You were created for Him, intended to think like Him and do things His way because you are created in His image. So, if a choice affects only your life and we make a bad one, one that is not aligned with God's heart of love, then you sin against Him and against yourself.

When your decisions involve others, and to be honest we must acknowledge that most of the choices you make involve others, like a stone thrown into a pond there are ripple effects of your choices and actions. So whenever you do something that is not in keeping with God's heart, or His way of thinking and His will, it is what the Bible calls sin. Whenever you make these kinds of choices, there are consequences to yourself and to others.

Given that God is a Holy God whose very nature is all goodness and love, the only way you can come into His presence is the way He provided—through Christ. Apart from the sacrifice of Jesus, you could not live in the Father's presence with your sin nature. Thank God for His one and only beloved Son who represents Him 100 percent (Son of God) fully, and also represents you 100 percent fully (Son of Man).

He showed us how we can live as a son before the Father, He gave us the blueprint, without sin, by taking upon Himself at the cross, not only our sin, but also the terrible nature of sin (selfishness) that was at work within us. As a result, when we believe in Him and come to the Father in His name, we are granted access to fellowship with the Father, where we can know the joy of sharing with Him just as Jesus does.

My point is that everything we think, do, or say that is not in agreement with God's heart and mind is sin and has consequences. When our actions result in others being hurt or violated in any way—physically, emotionally, or mentally—that is a result of decisions that we have made, that is sin's consequences. *Although God is more than able to change our minds, He will not do it in the sense of making us robots.* He will not override the right He has given each of us to choose and make own decisions.

If He had not given us that right, He would be labeled a monster who *makes* people do what He wants them to do. He would not be a loving Father because He would be *making* people do what He wanted them to, rather than giving them the right to choose, making decisions based on what is in their own mind and heart to do. Because we are free to make choices, good or bad, many terrible things can happen as a result.

Where Is God When Terrible Things Happen?

Is God near when terrible things happen? Of course He is. He is there before that action or choice took place and had been working tirelessly to help us make the right decisions. He put people in our way; He arranged all sorts of little things to get our attention. He probably tried to speak to us through others around us. We may even have had dreams or thoughts and other things trying to get our attention. God will put things in the way to try and thwart or hinder us from making the wrong choices—but in the end, the only thing He will *not* do is change our minds without our hearts' consent.

The most important thing for us to do is agree with Him about what He has said and done for us. That is the first thing, which is then followed by choosing to act in agreement with His loving nature. God even enables and strengthens us to make the right choices through His grace toward us and His faith within us. In spite of the fact bad things often happen as a result of our choices, we are often tempted to think that God is somehow responsible, or just "off the job," when they happen.

> ## God is always with you!

God is always with you. He was as close to you as possible and just as close to the perpetrator without making them think or do anything other than what they had chosen to do. Now I understand that you might think God's apparent lack of intervention is a terrible thing. But the truth is He intervenes in every way that He possibly can *without* violating anybody's right to choose! He does not want to dominate, manipulate, or control you in a wrong way. That surely is love. Needless to say, when you think about terrible things that happen, you find this hard to accept. But all things that are outside of His love and the way He thinks are terrible, and all of them have some adverse effects and consequences to others—but nonetheless *He is always with you.*

WHERE ARE YOU?

If you were to ask the Father, "Where are You?" in the midst of all the desperate situations that take place, He would say, "I am right here, not just watching over you, but bearing the pain, grief, hurt, and violation that you are and have endured."

How is that possible, you might ask? It's possible because Jesus Himself experienced every pain, grief, hurt, and violation, with all their consequences, as He walked through His life to the cross, and upon the Cross. There was no type of human pain that Jesus did not carry and experience in some way.

Your experiences were and are indeed very painful and real. Yet the truth is, He went through them with you and took them upon Himself in your place. He understands and knows the kind of pain and grief that you are carrying. He experienced the desolation, rejection, and loneliness that you feel. He has been there, not for Himself but for *you.* Therefore, when you come to Him, He knows exactly what you are going through; not only does He sympathize and empathize with you, but you can give it all over to Him. He has already carried it for you all the way to Calvary.

Jesus does *not* want you to be imprisoned by the things that have happened in your life and live with the pain of it forever. He does *not* want you to be tortured by emotional pain and hurtful memories. He paid a great price so that you could bring all that you have gone through and endured, along with all the pain and hurt, all the emotions and feelings you carry, and give them to Him. He endured the cross and carried your pain so you could understand that He came to die in your place, and to take your sin upon Himself. He does *not* want you to carry this weighty burden any longer. Give it all completely over to Him.

> **Give all your hurts, pain, and troubles to God—**
> **He wants to lighten your load.**

He has carried it (see Isa. 53). He has taken it. It is removed and taken away forever. You no longer need to be plagued or hurt by these things. You can be free. As you come to Him, He exchanges your pain and hurt, He relieves you from the weight of sin and grief for a new life, the life of His Spirit. In His great love, He not only takes away the old but gives you the new.

I explain it like this: I love my three children more than words could possibly express. I want everything that is wonderful for them, the best that can be. I don't want them to carry hurts, be in pain, persecuted, hated, or have a difficult life. I don't want anything less than the very best God has for them in this life.

I have raised them up to the best of my ability with His help and with the help of my wife. We have talked together, walked together, seen and done wonderful things together. We have also had various challenges and difficulties that we have come through. Our children know Jesus for themselves. They have learned to know Him through His Word and have personally seen His goodness toward them constantly.

We have prayed for them, taught them, and brought them up in the best way we could. Regardless of all the efforts we have made, despite the fact that we have done the very best for them that we can do; despite the fact that we have helped them and want to see them succeed in all they do; despite the fact that they know the Father and Jesus for themselves and have read His Word, *in the end, they have the God-given right to choose exactly what they want to do in and with their lives. That is their God-given right—to choose.* It's not up to me or their mother or any other person in their lives to make decisions. *It's their right.*

When I begin to try and make them think *my* way, see *my* way, respond *my* way, do things *my* way, when I try to *make* them love, when I attempt to make them into my own image or force them to behave the way I want—when I do that, I am in big trouble! That is called manipulation, control, and dominance, and it is a spirit of witchcraft. I have no right to do that. Their lives are not mine to live—*their lives are their own.* I may want to intervene and make them do things my way, but it is not the right thing to do.

WHY DOESN'T GOD INTERVENE?

This must be how it is for the Father in Heaven. Of course He could do and make many things happen, and we may often think that we want Him to make things happen for us. But do we? Would you really be grateful if He suddenly controlled and manipulated your life into loving Him, or wanting to follow Him? Would you really prefer it if He suddenly ran over your own thoughts making you think His own?

Now magnify that by millions of people. *There is no doubt in my mind that it would not be long before we were calling Him names, blaspheming Him, and accusing Him of interfering in our lives against our will.*

You might think, *Well He could have done it differently for my situation, after all what I have gone through is terrible. Surely a God of love would not allow these things.* Please remember—He doesn't "just allow" anything. He was right there. Perhaps this is your accusation against Him? Think of all of the terrible and awful situations you have heard about in the past week. No doubt some of them were unthinkable. Except that someone *did* think them! And it wasn't God! Then think of that multiplied millions of times over, again and again, because if God has to change the mind of one person committing a terrible act, then He has to do it with every person committing every terrible act over all of time. Beyond all this, we must consider not only our actions, but also the source of them.

More Than Actions

More than just the things we do, beyond our actions or the way we look at things, God (the Three in One) is love. He is purity itself. He is holy. He is perfect. He sees everything whether it's an act, a deed, or even a thought. If it is not something that is in line with His own heart and mind and in accordance with the way that He would act, then it is sin. Sin cannot enter His presence. So a sinner cannot enter into fellowship with God in any way. His own righteousness will never be sufficient, because just one thought is enough to cause sin. That is why the Bible so clearly states *"all have sinned," "all have gone their own way."* Each one of us is no better than the rest.

The Sin Bin

Thank God for Jesus who came to become our sin, taking our sins and trespasses away forever. He trashed them. He took them away just like your trash man takes away your garbage and you don't see it again—unless you go looking. He has done it. It is finished.

Health Warning

Even your thoughts can have terrible consequences. You can actually damage your physical health by making wrong decisions. In spite of potentially dire consequences, in His great love God has given you the right of free will, the right to choose, the right to decide. He will not make you do anything or be anyone. He loves you too much to make you into someone or something you do not want to be. He loves *you* too much to make you love or follow Him. *He loves you too much to make your decisions for you!*

So, He is not only working in all the situations around you, without changing and making up your mind for you, but He has actually visited every situation before it ever occurred and supplied the healing and wholeness that you needed to get up and on in life. *You are not meant to merely survive but to overcome,* and God's great love makes this possible for any who will receive it.

INCREDIBLE, REDEEMING LOVE

The incredible thing is that, God, in His redeeming love, reaches down to pick up the pieces of every life shattered by the consequences of sin. Through Jesus, He not only redeems the "mess," of our lives, even when it is caused by others, but also delivers us, heals us, and makes us completely whole. He sent His only Son to die for each of us, taking the place of our sinful selves on the cross. He was raised from the dead by the Father and stood before Him declaring to all of Heaven that He had redeemed us from every curse, sin, and transgression, making a way for us to receive the same blessing that He Himself received from the Father. So everything that Jesus had done was legally made ours and we can receive all that the Father has for us beginning today. And beyond that, we can become a channel of His blessing on the earth to others!

HOW GOD WORKS IN A FALLEN WORLD

Just as the Father worked through Jesus, who gave His life totally over to His will, anyone who believes in the Lord Jesus and in all He did upon the cross can *choose* to say *yes* to Him and align themselves with His heart, will, and purpose. Of course even though we are Christians, we still sometimes think and choose wrongly, making bad choices. When we align ourselves with Him and turn from our selfish ways, then He is able to teach us His ways, showing us by the Holy Spirit who dwells within us. He gently guides us about how we should walk, how we should live, what we should and shouldn't do. Even though we continue to sin, we are able to come to the Father through Jesus and ask His forgiveness.

Many people believe that it is enough if they go to church or read the Bible, which is, indeed, pleasing to the Father. But the thing that pleases Him the most is when we *choose* of our own free will, that God-given gift, to love and follow Him, seeking to be like Him, making the right decisions. Choosing to follow Him has the power to change the world.

JUST IMAGINE

Imagine if all people chose to follow Him—it would cause amazing things to happen worldwide. Indeed, this is what often happens when people choose to follow Him. When their friends, family, and neighbors see and are affected by this, many of them begin to change the way they think and live. I realize that this is not always true, because those who have chosen to live their own way and do their own thing, often persecute others who have chosen to live for God, but in many cases it is true, and in that micro environment of their life it can make a huge difference in the way people live. *What an amazing world it would be if people lived like Jesus!*

Always Working

I believe that the Father, Jesus, and the Holy Spirit are moving, working, and serving people, both Christian and non-Christian, at all times. *They are doing everything They can to bring love and truth into the hearts of Their children.* They dispatch angels, send messengers, and cause those who follow Them to become servants to those who do not yet know Them. I believe that They are moving in the affairs of humankind all the time. What They are *not* doing is *making* people believe, *making* them choose Him and His ways, or *making* them do things that they do not want to do. They would never do this, because this would not be love. The most important decision anyone can ever make is to know the Father—after that there are many other choices to make; choices that He is always there to help us make in time of need.

Placing the Blame

It's time to choose to thank God for your gift of free will, to be grateful for your ability to choose and do what you desire. It's also time to take responsibility for the choices and decisions you make. Everyone will have to account for what they have done. There is no point in blaming everybody else for the bad choices you have made. If you are blaming others for their bad choices, then you must also think about taking the blame for your choices because they might also be bad, even if to a lesser degree. It is not a question of the "degree of badness"; if they are not good choices, they fall short of God's choices! Non-Christians spend time blaming God and the government for all the evils of the world, and most Christians spend more time blaming the devil and fighting him than they do making right choices and loving the Father. It's time to grow up and take responsibility for your decisions, beginning with the most important one.

IT'S UP TO YOU

Have you made the most important decision of your life? It's up to you. What if you don't make the choice to love and follow Him? God cannot deny Himself, He still loves you. He will always love you; in fact, He can't stop loving you. He loves you so much He will continue to tell you, sending you messages in every way He can. He will never give up on you. He will never forsake you. He is for you, with you, and His love is toward you. He thinks good thoughts about you, and even when you do things that are not in agreement with His heart or mind, He still carries on loving you.

Of course as with every decision and every choice, there are always consequences. What God has said concerning such consequences will come to pass. However, His love is so great and far-reaching, He is so long-suffering, so kind, and so compassionate always working in every way possible for your best—simply look at Jesus, and you will see how the Father is.

He loves you so very much. It's up to you to decide. The blueprint for your life is before you. All you have to do is *choose* this day the *life* that He has for you.

God loves you so very much.

He thinks thoughts of peace and hope about you.

There is no evil in Him toward You.

He has a future and a destiny for you.

When you acknowledge Him as Savior and Lord, He gives you

a new heart, a new spirit and the Holy Spirit within.

He pours out His love upon You.

This love is the selfless love of God.

He is the foundation of your life.

He desires to build you, establish you, and make you strong.

As He walks with you, He teaches and disciplines you.

He gives gifts to help build and bring you to maturity.

He orders your life from what is the very least so you

can become great, so you become like He is—a master

craftsman, building up God's people.

This is what He is doing today.

All you have to do is choose to follow the blueprint for your life.

Chapter Sixteen

THE TESTAMENT—
THE WILL OF JESUS

The following is written as an overview of what God has done for you. Of course the New Testament is the full version, but this extract is meant to enthuse and excite you about God's eternal love for you. Feel free to write in your name.

**This New Covenant-New Testament, made before
the foundation of the world**

(See Ephesians 1)

between

Jesus Christ (the one and only begotten Son of the Father)

and

His Father God

This is a legally binding, unbreakable obligation between the named parties, based on unconditional love sealed by blood and sacred oath.

By entering into and satisfying the obligations of this New Covenant, the obligations of the Old Covenant are also fulfilled. Therefore the promises given in both covenants belong to the testator—Jesus Christ, the one and only beloved of the Father, who gives them freely to all those who choose to love and follow Him.

Witnessed in Heaven by:

❖ The Father

❖ The Word (before He came to the earth)

❖ The Holy Spirit

> *For there are three that bear witness in heaven: the Father, the Word, and the Holy Spirit; and these three are One* (1 John 5:7).

Whereas:

The Son of the Father, Jesus Christ, in full agreement and total submission to the Father, has promised to bear the sins of the whole world and pay the full penalty of that sin in His own being and body, giving Himself sacrificially and completely in order that sin be put away, and that all those who call upon the name of Jesus will be saved, adopted by the Father, becoming coheirs with Jesus His Son, receiving freely of all that is given to Him in the Father.

All the promises of God stated within are Yes, and in Him, Amen. (Let it be so.)

PROMISES OF GOD

1. Jesus

Now, it is therefore agreed and binding as follows:

Jesus the one and only begotten of the Father (see John 3:16) will be:

(a) Despised and rejected.

(b) A Man of sorrows and acquainted with grief.

(c) Despised and not esteemed.

(d) The bearer of the grief and sickness of humankind.

(e) The carrier of the sorrows of pain of humankind.

(f) Wounded for humankind's transgressions.

(g) Bruised and crushed for humankind's iniquities.

(h) Chastised, and by the blows and stripes against Him, He will bring peace, healing, and wholeness.

(i) Covered with the iniquity of humankind laid upon Him. (See Isaiah 53.)

(j) Led like a lamb to the slaughter.

(k) Humbled, obedient to the point of death, even the death of the cross.

> *For where there is a testament, there must also of necessity be the death of a testator* (Hebrews 9:16).

Because of this, the Father has given the Son His life and His full authority, and by the power of the Holy Spirit Jesus the Son, will be resurrected from the dead and will sit at the right hand of the Father. He will be highly exalted and given the name which is above every name.

And this deed and testament is signed and sealed by His own precious blood.

> *Not with the blood of goats and calves, but with His own blood He entered the most Holy place once for all, having obtained eternal redemption* (Hebrews 9:12).

> *"It is finished!"* (John 19:30)

> *...one of the soldiers pierced His side with a spear, and immediately blood and water came out* (John 19:34).

2. Jesus and You

It is also agreed and binding as follows:

> *...that whoever calls on the name of the Lord Jesus Christ shall be saved* (Acts 2:21).

For:

> *If you confess with your mouth the Lord Jesus and believe in your heart that God has raised Him from the dead, you will be saved* (Romans 10:9).

(a) And I,_____, child of God, have
now become one with Christ. And accordingly to the Testament that Jesus and the Father have made together, everything that belongs to Jesus now belongs to me,
_____ a coheir together with Christ.

(b) I,_____, willingly and gladly receive in
Jesus' precious name, all of these promises (and those written in the Testament) and will endeavor to seek first His Kingdom and His righteousness, that these might automatically be released into my own life and the life of my family.

For the promise is to you and to your children, and to all who are afar off, as many as the Lord our God will call (Acts 2:39)

3. You

Therefore I agree, acknowledge, confess, and declare the following:

(a) I,_____, am a child of God.

The Spirit Himself bears witness with our spirit that we are children of God (Romans 8:16).

(b) I _____ am a child of God.

And because you are sons, God has sent forth the Spirit of His Son into your hearts... (Galatians 4:6).

(c) I,_____, am a child and also an heir of
God, and the inheritance of Jesus is shared with me.

...and if a son, then an heir of God through Christ. ...heirs of God and joint heirs with Christ... (Galatians 4:7 and Romans 8:17).

(d) I,_____, am a totally new creation in
Christ, and old things have passed away.

Therefore, if anyone is in Christ, he is a new creation; old things have passed away, behold, all things have become new (2 Corinthians 5:17).

(e) I,_____, have a new heart, a new spirit, have been given the Holy Spirit and am enabled to walk in His Word and in His ways.

> *I will give you a new heart and put a new spirit within you.... I will put My Spirit within you and cause you to walk in My statutes...* (Ezekiel 36:26-27).

(f) I,_____, have been given a new spirit and my heart has been filled with Your love.

> *...the love of God has been poured out in our hearts by the Holy Spirit who was given to us* (Romans 5:5).

(g) I,_____, have been healed and made whole by the blood and stripes that were laid on Jesus as He carried my sorrows, grief, and pain to the cross.

> *who Himself bore our sins in His own body on the tree, that we, having died to sins, might live for righteousness—by whose stripes you were healed* (1 Peter 2:24).

(h) I _____ also receive the peace of Jesus, which is a peace beyond all earthly understanding.

> *Peace I leave with you, My peace I give to you...* (John 14:27).

(i) I,_____, receive the thoughts that You are thinking about me, thoughts that are good, beautiful and right.

> *For I know the thoughts that I think toward you...thoughts of peace and not of evil, to give you a future and a hope* (Jeremiah 29:11).

(j) I, _____, welcome my future, and the things You have prepared for me.

For we are His workmanship, created in Christ Jesus for good works, which God prepared beforehand that we should walk in them (Ephesians 2:10).

(k) I, _____, will never again be hope-less.

...to give you a future and a hope (Jeremiah 29:11).

(l) I, _____, will experience no lack or want as You are My Father.

The Lord is my Shepherd, I shall not want (Psalm 23:1).

(m) I, _____, have been given all things to live a godly and good life.

as His divine power has given to us all things that pertain to life and godliness... (2 Peter 1:3).

(n) I, _____, will always have enough, be-cause my God is a God of more than enough (El Shaddai) not just enough, and always has some left over (see John 6:11-13).

(o) I, _____, will never be forsaken or forgotten.

...I will never leave you nor forsake you (Hebrews 13:5).

(p) I, _____, receive all the promises in faith, and by that same faith, which is from Him and through Him, will taste and see in the days to come the re-ality and manifestation of all the above.

4. Witnessed on earth:

A New Covenant-New Testament between Jesus Christ the Darling of Heaven and His Father.

By:

(a) The Spirit (see 1 John 5:8)

(b) The water:

of life (see John 3:5)

of death (see John 19:34)

(c) The blood:

of life (see Deuteronomy 12:23)

of death (see John 19:34)

I am the Mighty One, I save you.
I rejoice over you with gladness,
I quiet you with My love,
I rejoice over you with singing.
—Father (see Zephaniah 3:17)

I was beside the Father as a Master Craftsman;
and I was daily His delight,
Rejoicing always before Him
Rejoicing in His inhabited world,
And My delight was with the sons of men.
—Jesus (see Proverbs 8:30-31)

...however, when He the Spirit of truth has come,
He will guide you...He will speak and
tell you of things to come...He will teach you...
and He will help you.
—Jesus speaking about the Holy Spirit (see John 16:5-15)

...and We will come to you and make our home with you (John 14:23).

ABOUT THE AUTHOR

Paul Graham Hubbard and his wife, Kjersti, have three children, Joshua, Maria, and Rebecca. Paul and his family live in Bradford, United Kingdom, and he oversees Christian Life Church in Bradford, as well as many other related churches globally.

He regularly travels to Nepal, Kenya, Italy, Norway, the United States of America, and other countries. He has been in full-time ministry for over twenty-five years. He is a divisional chaplain in the West Yorkshire Police Force. He is also an author.

To contact the author, please feel free to use the following e-mail address: office@christianlifechurch.co.uk or visit the Christian Life Church Website at www.christianlifechurch.co.uk.

Additional copies of this book and other book
titles from DESTINY IMAGE™ EUROPE
are available at your local bookstore.

We are adding new titles every month!

To view our complete catalog online, visit us at:
www.eurodestinyimage.com

Send a request for a catalog to:

Via Acquacorrente, 6
65123 - Pescara - ITALY
Tel. +39 085 4716623 - Fax +39 085 9431270
info@eurodestinyimage.com

"Changing the world, one book at a time."

Are you an author?

Do you have a "today" God-given message?

CONTACT US

We will be happy to review your manuscript
for the possibility of publication:

publisher@eurodestinyimage.com
http://www.eurodestinyimage.com/pages/AuthorsAppForm.htm